T0188480

Executive's Guide to Cyber Risk

Executive's Guide to Cyber Risk

Securing the Future Today

SIEGFRIED MOYO

WILEY

For general information on our other products and services or for technical support, please contact our Customer Care Department within the United States at (800) 762-2974, outside the United States at (317) 572-3993 or fax (317) 572-4002.

Wiley also publishes its books in a variety of electronic formats. Some content that appears in print may not be available in electronic formats. For more information about Wiley products, visit our web site at www.wiley.com.

Library of Congress Cataloging-in-Publication Data

Names: Moyo, Siegfried, author.
Title: Executive's guide to cyber risk : securing the future today / Siegfried Moyo.
Description: First edition. | Hoboken, New Jersey : Wiley, [2022] | Includes bibliographical references and index.
Identifiers: LCCN 2022013196 (print) | LCCN 2022013197 (ebook) | ISBN 9781119863113 (cloth) | ISBN 9781119863137 (adobe pdf) | ISBN 9781119863120 (epub)
Subjects: LCSH: Data protection. | Computer security. | Computer networks—Security measures. | Management information systems. | Computer crimes—Risk assessment.
Classification: LCC HF5548.37 .M68 2022 (print) | LCC HF5548.37 (ebook) | DDC 658.4/78—dc23/eng/20220525
LC record available at https://lccn.loc.gov/2022013196
LC ebook record available at https://lccn.loc.gov/2022013197

Cover Design: Wiley
Cover Image: © ismagilov/Getty Images
SKY10034674_060822

To everyone around the globe—no matter where they are—who are tirelessly working toward creating a cyber-secure future starting today.

Contents

Foreword

CYBERSECURITY IS, IN MY mind, one of the most serious issues facing the sustainability of the global economy, institutions, and society at large. Everyone, and increasingly everything, is connected through information technology. Our everyday life activities are dependent upon technology. Working from home and on the move has exacerbated the vulnerability of our platforms and poses significant challenges to CISOs that technology alone cannot solve.

Today, our digital technology systems are under attack from rogue hackers, cybercriminal gangs, and nation-sponsored cyber terrorists. No one is immune. Banks, hospitals, schools, and city governments are hacked; emails are compromised; and even the CIA has been hacked. And cybersecurity is critical to our ability to successfully tackle climate change, food scarcity, poverty, and global stability.

Most cybersecurity detection and prevention efforts concentrate on technology solutions as the primary line of defense. While information technology professionals are constantly upgrading their knowledge and cyber defense skills, many business executives, managers, and employees have a rudimentary understanding of what constitutes effective cybersecurity. This book aims to change that.

Siegfried Mayo is a hands-on cybersecurity professional deeply concerned about the lack of cybersecurity awareness and skills in today's global businesses. Like myself, he believes that every employee, and especially board directors and executives, needs to step up and take active accountability for protecting themselves and their organization. But accountability requires awareness, not just of the technical issues involved, but the organizational, infrastructure, and cultural issues that are the backbone of a cyber-safe organization.

This book is written especially for board directors and executives to help improve their understanding, awareness, and ability to effectively manage cybersecurity risks. After a short introduction to cybersecurity, chapters focus on understanding cyber risk, the importance of a well-crafted and communicated cybersecurity strategy, and the cultural and business factors that enable enterprise-wide cybersecurity.

Irrespective of your level of understanding of cybersecurity, this book will give you a holistic view of cyber risk management from a business perspective.

—Christiane Wuillamie, OBE
CEO, PYXIS Culture Technologies, Ltd.

Preface

THE PURPOSE OF THIS BOOK

In this book, I describe what I believe to be the five fundamental cyber risk management precepts that are critical for any organization business executive to understand to achieve their business goals and objectives. We are in an era of increasingly successful cyber-attacks that allow cybercriminals or hackers to steal, manipulate, or destroy critical data, or disrupt business operations by compromising critical infrastructure in businesses. To fight successfully against malicious intent, it's imperative that executives understand fundamental principles at a high level so they can prioritize cyber risk like any other business risk.

The goal of this book is to explain these five foundational precepts in non-technical terms so that the members of the Board of Directors (BOD) and C-Level executives (C-LEs) can continue to help their businesses prosper despite this era of ongoing cyber-attacks.

As I reflect on the past decade, every organization of any size, or industry of any magnitude, be it public or private, has been exposed to fear that's characterized by uncertainty and a possibly bleak future. Economic challenges are driven by the proximity of market forces and by cyber risks that expose the organization to undue spontaneous cyber-attacks that exploit the organization.

The world of cyber-attackers is not sitting still. Daily, organizations face a whole new set of cyber-attacks, some of which may not even yet exist. Currently, there is often a lack of focus in organizations that employ the support of the BOD, the shareholders, and the executives, as they might not have adequate comprehension of the basic precepts of cyber risk management but do have a direct impact on the organization's vision, objectives, and goals.

In a world of faster technology cycles and instant digitalization, board members and executives need to be more agile, collaborative, and forward-looking in regard to cyber risk management. Leaders of organizations should be able to articulate the basic and intrinsic knowledge of cyber risk management within the business realm or in their purviews.

There is an urgent need for the leaders of every organization to understand the key aspects of cyber risk management. Such knowledge is critical to an organization's future and ongoing success. Every organization needs forward-thinking precepts in order to achieve its vision and ease its decision-making in relation to cyber risk management. This is where *Executive's Guide to Cyber Risk: Securing the Future Today* comes into play. This book aims to explain the cyber risk management principles that organizations need to achieve business goals.

The book provides important fundamental cyber risk management precepts for board members, business executives, founders of start-ups, and owners of small- to medium-sized businesses. The key is identifying the gap between your current level of comprehension and what else you need to comprehend for better alignment on cyber risk management. This book helps to elucidate that gap.

Despite the existence of increasingly complex and sophisticated cyber-attacks, I have full confidence that board members, business executives, founders of start-ups, and business owners can achieve sustainable business growth when they understand the five foundational cyber risk management precepts.

 ## MY PERSPECTIVE

As an executive, it's important that you approach potential cyber risks with foresight and a forward-looking mindset. Otherwise, cyber risks will continue to incapacitate or harm your organization. This can go so far as to harm the global economy, public health, and overall safety. There are five fundamental cyber risk management precepts and strategies that I consider essential and relevant to board members, business executives, and business managers. They allow executives to get better aligned on cyber risk management within the organization. The precepts empower people with mindset-changing principles to mitigate potentially crippling cyber risk issues.

The change in mindset is from hindsight to foresight.

- ▓ Hindsight: Dealing with and understanding a problem only after it has happened.
- ▓ Foresight: The ability to judge correctly what is going to happen in the future and plan your actions based on this knowledge.

I am determined to help organizations develop foresight when it comes to cyber risks. Raising awareness is necessary and will bring about change, making the world more cyber-secure. I do not hesitate to share my points of view throughout this book. I think this increases the authenticity and value that I can give. I recognize that for some, the precepts may call into question my credibility. I'm afraid I must disagree, but I appreciate that this will be easier to read for those already committed to securing the future. I hope others will find it stimulating and valuable as well. My perspective on these fundamental five precepts has developed over many years, and it is my opinion that adopting these precepts will help build a cyber-secure future.

 ## WHAT THIS BOOK IS AND WHAT IT'S NOT

This book is not meant to substitute for or discredit any information security and cybersecurity standards or best practices, laws, or regulations. It's not intended to replace or undermine the great work being done by CISOs and cybersecurity professionals across the world, working to secure the organizations they have been entrusted to help. If you are reading this book with the intention of acquiring the skills to be certified in cybersecurity or information security, I am sorry to let you know you are in the wrong place. The book is not a training reference for any certification.

This book outlines five cybersecurity precepts or strategies for board members and executives, so they can develop foresight into cyber risk management. The book is for:

- Executives, so they can go forward better aligned with their cybersecurity executives.
- BOD members and executives, as a single reference guide that is a starting point to be able to identify and articulate the gaps in executive support.
- Founders of start-ups and owners and executives of small- to medium-sized organizations that don't have a clue where to start on cyber risk management.
- Anyone who wants to understand cyber risk better and wants to be part of shared social responsibility to make the future more cyber-secure.

This book should complement the work of the CISOs and cybersecurity professionals. They allow for business growth by incorporating diverse cyber risk management frameworks, and they work relentlessly with executives to help them comprehend cyber risk management in non-technical jargon to improve decision-making.

I recognize the limits of my perspective, but its validity as well. I do not claim any particular relevance because of my experience, and, despite my best efforts, I know that I likely have exhibited some biases along the way. But I believe that likelihood does not stop me from sharing my insights and knowledge to help move us toward a more cyber-secure world. If I were to allow this to keep me from sharing my perspectives, I would succumb to the neutrality trap. I hope readers will be open to what I have to say and keep my perspective in mind.

 ## HOW THE BOOK IS ORGANIZED

I organized this book into five chapters:

- Chapter 1, "Cyber Strategy," takes a strategy-centric approach to discussing cyber risk.
- Chapter 2, "Cyber Value," takes a value-centric approach to discussing cyber risk.
- Chapter 3, "Cyber Compliance," takes a compliance-centric approach to discussing cyber risk.
- Chapter 4, "Cyber Culture," takes a human-centric approach to discussing cyber risk.
- Chapter 5, "Cyber Resilience," takes a technology-centric approach to discussing cyber risk.

I expect that between today and the book's publication, new cyber risks will impact organizations, and they will shed new perspectives on the cyber risk management precepts I share in this book. I want this book to be part of a dynamic, ongoing discussion, and I hope it joins board members, executives, founders, and owners of organizations into a dialogue that I believe is critical to securing the future today.

Acknowledgments

THIS BOOK DRAWS ON two different streams of my life experiences—the spiritual and professional.

Spiritually: Thank you to the Lord Jesus Christ, my cornerstone, my strength, my fortress, for the gift of life, every second on earth up to this day, which has let me write the book and get to this stage of giving back through my profession.

Professionally: Thank you to all my professional colleagues, who challenged my mental models and thought processes, making me constantly strive to be a better person than I was the days or hours before. Both the positive and negative insights and feedback were essential to my growth and understanding.

I especially want to thank the contributors who worked with me over the months, providing objective feedback, challenging my mental models and thought processes, and supporting me as a first-time author. These include:

- Christiane Wuillamie, OBE and CEO of PYXIS Culture
- John Childress, chairman, PYXIS Culture Technologies Ltd
- Anna Collard, SVP content strategy and evangelist at KnowBe4 Africa
- Jack Jones, award-winning CISO, author of the FAIR standard, and the chairman of the FAIR Institute
- Kevin L. Jackson - 2X *USA Today and WSJ*, Best-Selling Author / CEO, GC GlobalNet/COO, SourceConnecte/SVP, TNS/Adjunct Professor, Adj. Prof., Tulane University

I was blessed to be in capable hands throughout the development of my work on this book. Kezia Endsley, the editor from Wiley, provided consistently helpful, supportive, and timely feedback on the various versions of each part of this book. Lori Martinsek and Warren Hapke, copy editing team, provided invaluable commentary, editing, and citation checking and was always tactful but direct in pointing out some of my blind spots. I also want to thank the

Wiley team who grasped the value of this project and have been supportive (and flexible!) throughout—especially Sheck Cho, Susan Cerra, Samantha Wu, Manikandan Kuppan.

Finally, I want to thank my family for their unstinting support throughout, especially my son, who always pushes me to be a better man that he can look up to. Thank you to my father for his push and invaluable support. And my most special thanks to colleagues who were constantly willing to listen, support, distract, and entertain when necessary.

About the Author

Siegfried Moyo has grown within the information security industry from a junior security engineer to a leader of information security teams in organizations with a global footprint. He has experience working across different industries (including banking, manufacturing, technology, the public sector, and logistics and supply chain). He is a cybersecurity professional with over fifteen years of experience in information security. He has hands-on technical experience with diverse information security technologies.

He works toward increasing stakeholder value by providing cyber assurance and managing cyber risk across organizations and creating a robust and sustainable cybersecurity strategy that is resilient against multiple cyber threats. He is a trusted cybersecurity advisor on determining and establishing the right cybersecurity governance and security practices for organizations and helps business executives at the C-Suite level understand cyber risks.

He has practical experience in the following cybersecurity domains: cybersecurity resilience, cybersecurity governance, cybersecurity risk management framework, cybersecurity engineering, cybersecurity operations, cybersecurity strategy development/deployment, and cybersecurity enterprise architecture to align with business/enterprise objectives and goals.

He received a bachelor of science in cybersecurity and a master of science in cybersecurity from EC-Council University. He is currently pursuing a doctor of philosophy (PhD) in Cybersecurity Leadership at Capitol Technology University.

While writing this book, Siegfried lived in Madrid, Spain, with his family.

CHAPTER ONE

Cyber Strategy

The Strategy-Centric Approach

> Cybersecurity is the mission-focused and risk-optimized management of information which maximizes confidentiality, integrity, and availability using a balanced mix of people, policy, and technology while perennially improving over time.
>
> —Mansur Hasib, speaker, educator, career coach

 INTRODUCTION

What exactly is a cyber strategy? Let's start by defining strategy. The word "strategy" is derived from the Greek word *strategos*, which is a combination of two words—*stratia* (meaning army) and *ago* (meaning to lead or move). Merriam-Webster defines "strategy" as "a careful plan or method for achieving a particular goal, usually over a long period," or "the skill of making or carrying out plans to achieve a goal."[1]

A strategy is a course of action taken by management to achieve one or more of the organization's objectives. We may alternatively define strategy as "a broad direction established for the organization and its many components to reach a desired condition in the future."

A comprehensive strategic planning process yields a strategy. A strategy is all about integrating organizational operations and using and distributing corporate resources to fulfill current objectives. We do not build a plan in a vacuum; let's keep this in mind. Any action conducted by an organization is likely to elicit a response from those affected, whether they are competitors, customers, workers, or suppliers. We may also characterize strategy as knowing what we want to achieve, being aware of the unpredictability of events, and considering possible or actual actions. An organization's strategy explains its business, the economic and human organization it aims to be, and the impact it intends to make on its shareholders, customers, and society. So strategy is preparing a long-term plan that will guide an organization in achieving its objectives.

In "Strategic Planning for Public and Nonprofit Organizations," an article on the Insentra website, John M. Bryson defines strategic planning as:

A disciplined effort to produce fundamental decisions and actions which shape and guide what an organization is, what it does and why it does it—all with a focus on the future.[2]

 CYBERSECURITY STRATEGY

The European Union Agency for Cybersecurity (ENISA) defines cybersecurity strategy as:

A national cybersecurity strategy (NCSS) is a plan of actions designed to improve the security and resilience of national infrastructures and services. It is a high-level top-down approach to cybersecurity that establishes a range of national objectives and priorities that should be achieved in a specific timeframe.[3]

In essence, a *cybersecurity strategy* is an organization's plan to reduce business risk from cyber-attacks by maintaining confidentiality, integrity, and availability in all the organization's information systems and data.

The primary request of any organization or institution's Board of Directors (BOD) and C-level executives (C-LE) is for a robust, scalable, and agile cybersecurity strategy that enables business agility and sustainability. A robust cybersecurity strategy is critical for business operations as it protects against cyber risks and mitigates potential data breaches and other cyber threats to critical infrastructure and critical data. For a BOD member or a C-LE to be able to fathom the value proposition of the organization's cybersecurity strategy, there must be invested accountability on how business is aligned to the specific organization-level approach to cyber value, cyber compliance, cyber culture, and cyber resilience, but all of this starts from the strategy. All these are the precepts in the following chapters of the book.

THE VALUE PROPOSITION OF A CYBERSECURITY STRATEGY

Most executives' first thought is determining what the return on investment (ROI) is on investing in a cybersecurity strategy. The ROI is the total value of the cost of cyber breaches averted minus the cost of mitigating cyber risks. After reading the next chapter, you'll understand why this is often difficult to measure and learn how to calculate it better.

Beyond the ROI or net value, the absence or misalignment of a cybersecurity strategy will not enable the board of directors or C-level executives to take the subsequent business strategic risks that facilitate business growth and success in the foreseeable future. A cybersecurity strategy allows the organization to capture more value from its business model.

For example, suppose an organization's strategy is to grow through mergers and acquisitions (M&As). The cybersecurity strategy should mitigate any cyber risks that emerge with each new M&A while not losing focus on the current cyber risks. The organization's expansion and growth depend on the trust of existing and new consumers. The cybersecurity strategy should be in line with building the trust of its customers after the M&A-critical infrastructure and data are secure. A strategy in line with the business's objectives is the only assurance that enables the board of directors and C-level executives to take the business to the next level or the next innovative idea or concept. After that, executives can confidently answer the questions posed in this chapter.

The primary concern of any executive in this realm should be a successful cyber-attack or security breach. Cyber-attacks have caused significant damage to businesses, affecting the bottom line, their business standing, and customer and consumer trust.

THE EXECUTIVE'S ROLE IN CYBERSECURITY STRATEGY

You may wonder why a cybersecurity strategy should be the first foundational precept for the BOD and C-LEs, as prescribed in this book. Most organizations' executives are not treating cybersecurity like any other strategic business decision. For a cybersecurity strategy to enable the business effectively and successfully, it has to be driven by the organization's leadership. Cybersecurity strategy that has the support of executive leadership invites the actionable strategic-centric approach and governance model that gives the right priority to cyber risk management. Members of the BOD and C-LEs need to start asking the right questions about cybersecurity strategy to make sure sufficient investments are made to minimize business disruptions from cyber risks. A cybersecurity strategy that is well articulated by the executive leadership will automatically align business strategy objectives and organization risk appetite. Some of the implications of ignoring cybersecurity strategy are listed below:

- BOD and C-LE insecurities emerge from the lack of a cybersecurity strategy or plan to reduce cyber risks tailored to the organization's objectives and risk profile.
- BOD and CLE insecurities emerge due to the absence or misalignment of the cybersecurity strategy to business strategy. The lack of and misalignment results in crippling the business to be more innovative and remain sustainable for the foreseeable future despite operating in an era of increase in cyber-attacks.

If you are a member of the BOD or a C-LE of an organization, you need to be able to articulate answers to these questions:

- Does your organization have a cybersecurity strategy that's specific to the organization's core business?
- Is the organization's cybersecurity strategy aligned to the business goals?
- Does the cybersecurity strategy have adequate resources to mitigate risk within the organization's risk appetite and risk tolerance?
- Does the cybersecurity strategy have adequate financial support to manage cyber risks against the critical assets?
- Is the organization cyber-compliant with all laws and regulatory or industry-specific requirements?

- How does the organization's cybersecurity strategy ensure that it can avoid, respond to, and recover from constantly changing cyber threats?
- Has the organization integrated people, processes, and technology into its cybersecurity strategy?

The failure to clearly articulate a response to these and other questions invites business risk that would result in lost shareholder value, less consumer and customer trust, limited business growth, and more. No single strategy-centric approach to cybersecurity strategy is ideal for all business models; the cybersecurity strategy has to be one that suits your business. Given the rising prevalence of technology, software vulnerabilities, ransomware, and other vectors of cyber-attacks, this makes it imperative for cybersecurity strategy to be at the top of every executive's agenda. We live in a world of constant volatility, and if you have invested interest and support in how your organization's cybersecurity strategy will cope with the continual change of cyber-attacks, in both scale and complexity, you will enable your organization to archive its business goals while managing cyber risk within the organization's risk appetite. Cybersecurity strategy enables BOD members and C-LEs to recognize and have a high level of understanding of the potential impacts of and losses due to cyber risks, which have resulted in an impact on operations, reputations and revenues.

Potential Loss Due to Cyber Risks

Cyber-attacks can result in economic, reputational, and legal losses and problems. Let's look at each of these areas in more detail.

Economic Losses

Cyber-attacks often result in substantial financial losses arising from:

- Theft of corporate information
- Theft of financial information (e.g., bank details or payment card details)
- Theft of money
- A halt in business operations (e.g., inability to carry out transactions online)
- Loss of business or contracts

Damage to a Corporation's Reputation

Trust is an essential element of the customer relationship. Cyber-attacks can damage a business's reputation and erode the trust of consumers and customers. It might lead to:

- Loss of customers
- Decrease in sales
- Decrease in net revenue

Reputational damage can also affect suppliers and relationships with partners, investors, and other third parties vested in the business.

Legal Ramifications

Data protection and privacy rules require that the executives oversee the security of any personal data handled or stored, whether on internal or external systems. If this data is compromised (inadvertently or on purpose) and the company cannot implement cybersecurity controls, it may face regulatory penalties.

▣ EXECUTIVE'S GUIDE TO CYBERSECURITY STRATEGY

There is no strategy without accountability and there is no accountability without leadership.

—John R. Childress, Chairman, PYXIS Culture Technologies Ltd.

The "Executive's Guide" sections in this book, like this one, provide details and foundational knowledge for executives so they can make informed cost- and resource-effective investment decisions with their most senior cybersecurity executives, such as chief information security officers (CISOs), to limit the organization's cyber risk within the organization's risk appetite. Cybersecurity strategy is critical in enabling any organization to adopt a proactive approach to cyber risk management, as opposed to reacting to every new cyber-attack in hindsight, which can be costly and time-consuming. Whether an organization has an outdated cybersecurity strategy in place or is establishing its first one, executives can use these guide sections to understand why it is vital to support an effective and strategic cybersecurity plan.

Cybersecurity and Information Security

Cybersecurity is a popular topic these days, but what exactly does it mean? Cybersecurity refers to the collection of tools, policies, guidelines, risk-management techniques, activities, best practices, assurances, and technologies that companies use to secure the availability, integrity, and confidentiality of assets in linked infrastructures in government, private businesses, and individual settings.

These assets include connected computing devices, employees, infrastructure, applications, digital service providers, and citizens. The concept of cybersecurity is not as broadly accepted as that of information security. Some individuals believe the concepts are interchangeable or that cybersecurity is either a subset or superset of information security. Many believe that cybersecurity is simply a newer and perhaps more sophisticated version of traditional computer security, which is:

> The ability to protect or defend the use of cyberspace from cyber-attacks.
> —*National Institute of Standards and Technology (NIST)*[4]

This specific definition from the NIST does not talk about cyber risk and the need to deal with it. Cyber risk management is an essential aspect of prioritizing where an organization deploys the limited resources for its cybersecurity strategy.

A more straightforward and more helpful definition of a cybersecurity strategy is: "the actions, direct and indirect, an organization takes to reduce the risks of being connected to the Internet to a level acceptable to that organization."

According to the NIST, "Information security means protecting information and information systems from unauthorized access, use, disclosure, disruption, modification, or destruction to provide integrity, confidentiality, and availability." By protecting information from cyber threats, you achieve three goals:

▪ *Confidentiality*: You keep your secrets under control.
▪ *Integrity*: Data is not corrupted.
▪ *Availability*: You can see and use information whenever necessary.

Cybersecurity and Trust

One of cybersecurity's most popular terms is "zero trust." The use of the word *trust* in cybersecurity can be confusing. Here is one way to consider this concept, according to Palo Alto Networks:[5]

> Zero trust is a strategic approach to cybersecurity that secures an organization by eliminating implicit trust and continuously validating every stage of digital interaction. Rooted in the principle of "never trust, always verify," zero trust is designed to protect modern environments and enable digital transformation.

Cyber Risk Management

To clear any confusion on how the cybersecurity strategy and cyber risk management are related, the NIST[6] outlines that "risk management is a fundamental principle of cybersecurity. It is the basis of the NIST Framework for Improving Critical Infrastructure Cybersecurity. Agencies of the US Government certify the operational security of their information systems against the requirements of the FISMA Risk Management Framework (RMF). The alternative to risk management would presumably be a quest for total security—both unaffordable and unachievable."

There are various definitions of risk management from all the cybersecurity industry standards and publications. In this book, for purpose of alignment with the next chapter, we focus on the FAIR definition,

> Risk management is the process of achieving and maintaining an acceptable level of exposure to loss, within the context of an organization's objectives and constraints.
> —*Jack Jones, Cofounder and Chairman of FAIR*

Managing risks is a critical component of any business's cybersecurity strategy. Organizational systems, people, networks, and devices are all vulnerable. The business's services and operations and even its customers may be at risk. The more the business relies on a web presence, the more critical it is to identify and control the cyber risks that have the potential to impact the organization. Cyber threats—ranging from human errors to malicious attacks by hackers—can disrupt critical business operations or expose critical information. Cyber risk assessment involves identifying, analyzing, and evaluating potential risks. As part of the assessment, the organization should look at the entire organization as well as the culture to identify potential threats arising from, but not limited to:

- People, processes, and technologies
- Vulnerabilities within critical infrastructure and critical data
- Vulnerabilities from third-party partners

The key to effective cyber risk management that enables the BOD members and C-LEs to make informed decisions is having a risk appetite statement in place. The risk appetite statement is only defined and outlined by the BOD and C-LEs of an organization, A risk appetite statement firmly outlines the tone for the BOD's and C-LEs' approach to risk management. When the organization's appetite for risk is tied to business operations, compliance, culture, and reporting objectives, it is also more likely to fulfil its strategic business goals and objectives. The breadth of a risk appetite statement will always differ, depending on the organization. Cybersecurity strategy that is developed without a risk appetite statement is more costly, and cybersecurity measures are applied on almost everything and anything. After the clear outline by the BOD and C-LEs of the organization's risk appetite comes a clear decision on risk tolerance. For cybersecurity strategy investments in cyber risk management to be cost- and resource-effective, the BOD and C-LEs must have well-articulated and clearly defined statements specific to their organization on the two subjects discussed below: risk appetite and risk tolerance.

According to Reciprocity,[7]

Risk Appetite—Risk appetite pertains to a company's longer-term strategy concerning what goal it needs to achieve and the resources available to achieve it, expressed in quantitative terms. An organization's risk appetite indicates the amount of risk it's willing to accept to attain its business objectives.

Risk Tolerance—Risk tolerance, on the other hand, sets the acceptable minimum and maximum variation levels for a company, business unit, individual initiative, or specific risk category. A risk tolerance range for minimum and maximum levels of risk is usually set by the committee that oversees the organization's risk management strategy and is then approved by leadership.

A high level of risk tolerance means that an organization is willing to take a high risk, while a low level of risk tolerance means that the company isn't willing to accept any risks.

Before we proceed to the next steps, it is now clear that a risk appetite statement encourages consistent, risk-informed decision making aligned with strategic goals and solid corporate governance by establishing explicit risk-taking boundaries

NEXT STEPS/REFLECTION

Now we can revisit some of the questions posed earlier.

A Cybersecurity Strategy Aligned to the Business Objectives

Does your organization have a cybersecurity strategy that's specific to your organization's business? Is the organization's cybersecurity strategy aligned to the business's goals?

To determine if a cybersecurity strategy is appropriately aligned to an organization's business objectives, executives need to have a clear understanding of how cybersecurity strategy is enabling the organization's vision and goals within the organization's risk appetite. For example, say that your business goals are to increase market share through digitalization, with critical information processed or stored on the critical infrastructure, which means you need a bigger Internet presence or digitalization. The cybersecurity strategy needs to focus on a cyber-secure digitalization approach to the critical infrastructure and critical data. If web applications are not balanced with a comprehensive cyber risk management strategy that responds to related cyber threats, your organization cannot achieve its goals, let alone business growth.

Organizations can reference several existing frameworks (such as those of the NIST and ISO) to provide a foundation for building an organization's specific cybersecurity strategy. In this case, the BOD members and C-LEs would need to embrace a fact-based, data-driven mathematical approach that will empower them to comprehend the cyber risks posed to the organization, the likelihood that those risks could be exploited, and the possible commercial impact if a cyber-attack is successful. The fact-based approach (in the next chapter) will enable any BOD and C-LEs to evaluate, in monetary terms, the level of exposure to loss for the business due to cyber risk and to understand where resources should be allocated for the most cost-effective approach. This is done by delving deeper into the data, figures, and facts.

An Agile Cybersecurity Strategy That Can React to Changes

How does the organization's cybersecurity strategy ensure that it can avoid, respond to, and recover from constantly changing cyber threats?

Having a robust cybersecurity strategy is crucial, but the ability to pivot quickly, based on the external threat landscape, is equally important. And this is where company culture plays a big role. Organizations must ensure that their short-term plans and people are aware, capable, and agile enough to enable them to react to new and emerging threats and changes in the market. Every time an organization performs an assessment, they should have complete visibility into internal and external threats, while adjusting their cyber risk mitigation plans and recommendations accordingly.

Any organization that relies on Internet technologies or information is vulnerable to cyber risk. The risk relates to an organization's use, ownership, operation, engagement, impact, and Internet adoption. Cyber or IT risks may degrade business value and are frequently the result of having no plan or a misaligned plan to mitigate or manage the risks associated with technology or cyber risk classifications. Cyber risk spans a range of business-critical areas, such as:

- *Availability*: for example, failure to access IT systems required for company operations
- *Security*: for example, compromised organizational data because of unauthorized access or misuse
- *Performance*: for example, decreased productivity because of sluggish or delayed access to IT systems
- *Compliance*: for example, lack of compliance with laws and regulations (such as those for data protection)
- *Culture*: for example, whether employee behavior is either an enabler or a cyber risk management strength is critical to business success

Cybersecurity strategy is more than simply a cost of doing business. It has the potential to be the catalyst for the company's growth and success. This alignment must begin with a strong business case for cybersecurity investment, which turns into business outcomes and business value. Until recently, attempts to advertise cyber risk management strategy as an enabler have been clunky, where most organizations have focused on simplifying cybersecurity strategy or minimizing the integration into IT at an early point of the lifecycle to decrease cost and complexity. The issue is that this approach cannot resist the growing threat environment and the threat actors who operate inside it.

A Cybersecurity Strategy Supported from the Top Down

Has the organization integrated people, processes, and technology into its cybersecurity strategy?

Most executives only get involved when there is an significant cyber issue. It's time for executives to understand and develop a forward-looking cyber strategy that makes the organization more resilient to both current and potential cyber-attacks. Cybersecurity strategies can take many forms and can go into varying levels of detail, depending on the organization's objectives and levels of cyber-readiness.

This chapter envisages that executives will have a cybersecurity strategy as:

- ▓ An expression of the vision, high-level objectives, principles, and priorities that guide an organization in addressing cyber risks.
- ▓ A detailed overview of the stakeholders entrusted with strengthening cybersecurity, as well as their various roles and responsibilities as members of the BOD or C-LE team.
- ▓ A description of the steps, programs, and initiatives that an organization will undertake to protect its critical infrastructure and data, and in the process, improve its cybersecurity and cyber-resilience.

Once your organization has acknowledged that a cyber risk exists, you can begin to build a renewed cybersecurity strategy with built-in cyber resilience. Setting the vision, objectives, culture, and priorities up front enables organizations to approach cybersecurity holistically across the entire ecosystem, instead of at a particular sector or objective or in response to a specific risk.

Cybersecurity foresight is never perfect, but it is more useful than hindsight.
—*Christiane Wuillamie, OBE, Chief Executive of PYXIS Culture Technologies Ltd.*

Priorities for cybersecurity strategies vary by organization and industry. The focus for one may address critical infrastructure-related risks; for others, it may protect consumers or customer personal information or intellectual property, promote trust in the online environment, improve public cybersecurity awareness, or a combination of these issues. The need to identify and prioritize investments and resources is critical to successfully managing risks in an area as all-encompassing as cybersecurity.

Start-Ups, Small- and Medium-Sized Enterprises (SMEs)

Regardless of the size of the business, either a large enterprise or small- to medium-sized enterprise (SME), both are targets of cyber-attacks.

Large organizations have a larger cyber threat landscape than start-ups and SMEs because of the number of employees, amount of data, or infrastructure size. For start-ups and SMEs, developing a cybersecurity strategy is more critical than ever since cyber-attacks are now more disruptive.

The biggest cyber challenge for any start-up or SME is knowing where to start its cybersecurity strategy and what the best, most cost-effective way is to approach cyber risk management. Developing a cybersecurity strategy is a crucial first step in ensuring that the business is secure and resilient in the era of cyber-attacks. The absence of some form of cybersecurity strategy or even a framework to follow for a start-up or SME, especially when there is no or limited on-site cybersecurity expertise, makes it challenging to ensure that the business will remain sustainable for the foreseeable future.

Cybersecurity strategy should be established not only by large corporations. Start-ups and SMEs are not exempt from the destructive impact of hazardous cyber assaults. In most cases, the initial focus of any start-up and SME is how to increase revenue and market share, and how to generate leads and business growth. Start-up founders and SME executives often do not fathom the potential impact of cyber risks and disparage anything related to cybersecurity. The current situation places most start-ups and SMEs in a critical position. Currently most start-ups and SMEs are trying to manage cyber risk while usually not being skilled or equipped enough to internalize this process. Therefore, there is a need for a practical and easily applicable model to identify a business's cyber risk profile and its dynamics. Start-ups and SMEs are among the least mature and most vulnerable in cyber risk management and cybersecurity resilience.

Start-ups and SMEs must begin to give diligent and more focused approaches to cybersecurity strategy because the impact of potential cyber-attacks on a start-up or an SME is more catastrophic. It is a fair assumption that not every start-up and SME will be able to afford a CISO and a fully staffed cybersecurity team effectively to align the business's goals and objectives to its cybersecurity strategy. Malicious actors are fully aware of these limitations; thus, start-ups and SMEs will not be exempt from the growing number of cyber threats. The rise of cyber threats makes it imperative for the founders and executive teams of SMEs to evaluate cyber risks and have a strategy-centric approach to cybersecurity for more cost- and resource-effective investment decisions. The recommendation of this book for enhancing cybersecurity risk management is leveraging the one widely recognized cybersecurity framework (CSF) document by the US National Institute of Standards and Technology (NIST). The NIST CSF is a good place to start for any start-up or SME, since it offers a fundamental foundation that businesses can use to develop their overall cybersecurity. Through a CSF evaluation, organizations will effectively construct a baseline to build their cybersecurity strategy and a solid foundation for a practical assessment. NIST CSF provides guidelines, best practices, and standards for cybersecurity risk management. In the absence of a security professional or expert, the founders and executives of any start-up or SME need to have a high-level understanding of the NIST CSF. This will empower the founders and business executives of the start-ups and SMEs to clearly articulate the next step to bolstering a cybersecurity strategy, either by considering employing a managed security service provider (MSSP) for cyber risk management or by building an in-house capability through leveraging the NIST CSF. Although there is no one-size-fits-all approach to the cyber risk management plan, the fundamentals of an effective cyber risk management strategy apply across several sectors. The NIST CSF can help leaders develop a cybersecurity strategy that maps to their organization's specific and unique needs.

Ongoing cybersecurity strategy reevaluation among founders and SME executives will encourage leadership to take a more proactive approach to cyber risk mitigation. For effective management of cyber risk in today's constantly changing business and technical landscapes, start-up founders and SME executives will need to acquire and maintain a foundational understanding of cyber risk management and learn the latest knowledge and best practices through a strategic-centric approach to cybersecurity. As founders and business executives of start-ups and SMEs, you are fully responsible for securing your organization's critical infrastructure and critical information.

The NIST CSF is in Appendix A of this book for further reading for all start-up founders and SME executives. It is a starting point that lets you know how to engage service providers and why. The NIST CSF is also valid for a large organization that has adopted no specific cybersecurity frameworks.

SUMMARY

Organizations must change their mindsets by reevaluating policies, practices, culture, and technology and by identifying where a cybersecurity strategy is critical to growth and success. A good starting point is to understand the relationship between cybersecurity strategy and business, which enables straightforward decisions by the BOD and C-LEs on cyber risk management investments. Cybersecurity strategy also requires that it should be constantly realigned with business objectives, which can change at any time. A cyberse-curity strategy is critical to accomplishing economic goals, and it should reflect how those goals are enabled in the organization. This can be accomplished by referring to current business initiatives that strive to achieve digitalization or developmental goals and then evaluating how the cybersecurity strategy might be included.

Finally, developing a cybersecurity strategy should transform an organi-zation's culture with logical and implementable policies that will assist it in meeting its business objectives. Cybersecurity strategy should, at a minimum, cover the actions, programs, culture, and technology initiatives that should be implemented; the resources provided for those efforts; and how those resources should be used. Similarly, the process should determine the metrics that will guarantee meeting the shared objectives within the established budgets and timelines. The next chapter, "Cyber Value Risk: The Value-Centric Approach," enables businesses to describe their cyber risk exposure in monetary terms to better assess the risks and make business-informed decisions on cybersecu-rity investment priorities. Organizations can reliably calculate the financial impact of cyber risks such as data breaches, identity theft, critical infrastruc-ture outages, and many more with the help of the FAIR model. Cyber Value employs ways to shift from opinion-based to fact-based approaches that are more accurate. BOD members and C-LEs can better prioritize cyber invest-ments and promote alignment between cybersecurity strategy and overall risk management plan.

NOTES

1. https://www.merriam-webster.com/dictionary/strategy
2. https://www.insentragroup.com/us/insights/geek-speak/professional-services/the-art-of-advisory-services/
3. ENISA - https://www.enisa.europa.eu/topics/national-cyber-security-strategies

4. NIST - https://csrc.nist.gov/glossary/term/information_security
5. Palo Alto - https://www.paloaltonetworks.com/cyberpedia/what-is-a-zero-trust-architecture
6. NIST-https://www.nist.gov/system/files/documents/2016/09/16/s.lipner-b.lampson_rfi_response.pdf
7. Reciprocity - https://reciprocity.com/resources/whats-the-difference-between-risk-appetite-vs-risk-tolerance/#:~:text=Put%20simply%2C%20risk%20appetite%20is,organization%20is%20willing%20to%20tolerate

CHAPTER TWO

Cyber Value

The Value-Centric Approach

A risk management program cannot be considered mature or effective if it can't reliably measure risk. And here's some additional food for thought—which maturity model in our industry accounts for ANY of the points I've discussed in these two posts? None that I'm aware of. They all call for risk measurement and prioritization to take place and then assume that it's going to be done well. Clearly, this is a missed opportunity to fundamentally improve the efficacy of risk management programs.

—Jack Jones, author of the FAIR standard

 INTRODUCTION

The previous chapter explained how important it is to ensure that cybersecurity strategy enables business objectives. Since we now assume that the organization has a robust cybersecurity strategy, this chapter focuses on articulating the dollar value of mitigating cyber risk, and this chapter also attempts to answer some questions highlighted in the previous chapter. The second foundational precept, cyber value, enables you as a member of the BOD or a C-LE to build from the cybersecurity strategy and have information that helps the BOD and C-LEs have straightforward discussions in business language about dollars. Organizations can now reliably calculate the financial impact of cyber risks such as data breaches, identity theft, and critical infrastructure outages,

As in the previous chapter on cybersecurity strategy, the BOD and C-LEs expect robust cyber risk management that mitigates and reduces the organization's exposure to cyber risk to an acceptable level, based on the organization's risk appetite. We also established that the BOD and C-LEs define the risk appetite statements, which implies that cybersecurity and the rest of the business's organization must simultaneously determine what the most valuable assets or "crown jewels" are. If the crown jewels are not identified, it only results in costly cybersecurity investments that are not focused or value-centric, as the cybersecurity measures would then be applied on everything and anything. It is a fair assumption that in such situations, risk tolerance is also not defined. In this chapter, the cyber value precept addresses the next step of implementing a value-centric or focused approach based on the assumption that the first strategic-centric precept has already been adopted by the organization.

The financial impact of the COVID-19 pandemic will still weigh heavily on most organizations for the foreseeable future. As if organizations don't have enough to deal with, the increase in cyber-attacks during the COVID-19 pandemic exacerbated its economic impact on any business. It makes it more imperative to have a value-centric approach to cybersecurity. As a member of the BOD or a C-LE, you would agree that no organization has unlimited financial resources or capacity; thus, organizations require a method to prioritize cyber risk mitigation. The cyber value precept empowers the BOD and C-LEs to answer the fundamental question about financial strategy: How does cybersecurity create more value for shareholders? Cyber value (the value-centric approach). when integrated into the cybersecurity risk management process, enables organizations to correctly prioritize the cyber risk within acceptable levels and capacity.

In an era when every dollar counts, basing BOD and C-LE decisions about cybersecurity investment on opinions, assumptions, and qualitative labels will remain a costly approach. As highlighted in Chapter 1, the BOD and C-LEs can make informed decisions based on fact-based, data-driven mathematical approaches to cyber risk management. The value-centric approach will help business executives answer questions such as, "What is the ROI on cybersecurity investment?" When cyber risk management is conveyed in financial terms that every company stakeholder understands, it leads to better corporate decision making and cooperation.

All organizations or private or public enterprises are exposed to cyber-related loss (cyber risk), and these events must be communicated to the organization's executives. Most executives have three significant areas that need communication from their cybersecurity team:

- *Cyber risk status*: Bad news should not surprise them. The BOD members and C-LEs can invest in financial resources and call for support from other business functions.
- *Cyber risk analysis*: As owners of the enterprise risk, they need to make high-priority risk decisions that are timely and actionable.
- *Cyber risk posture*: They must communicate the organization's cybersecurity story to various employees and partners, sometimes on the spur of the moment.

UNDERSTANDING CYBER VALUE

Cyber value is the key principle; it is critical for any BOD member or C-LE to comprehend the financial ramifications of a significant cyber-attack at the leadership level through cyber risk quantification. Cyber value is fundamental as it empowers the BOD and C-LEs to make value-based decisions on cyber risk management investments that are aligned to business objectives.

Cyber risk quantification helps to enable cybersecurity risk management in any organization. When the BOD and C-LEs have a high-level understanding of cyber risk quantification, they will find it less complicated to analyze the organization's cyber risk. This understanding provides financial insight into the possible monetary loss resulting from a cyber incident.

The critical focus of cyber value is not on everything related to IT, but on the organization's most critical IT infrastructure and critical information that directly influences revenue or business operations. We sometimes refer to this critical infrastructure and information as the organization's "crown jewels." Crown jewels are the most valued assets of the organization, ones that are critical to achieving its business objectives.

A cyber risk management approach that is qualitative can have much ambiguity. Cyber risk quantification is a management technique. However, it is a complex process if it's not adopted well. Cyber risk calculations allow for discussions about the benefit of cybersecurity in terms that executives can comprehend. The complexity of this is that organizations frequently lack precise data about the cyber threats they potentially face, because their cybersecurity strategy is either missing or misaligned with their business objectives. This related issue was discussed in the previous chapter, which covers in more detail the absence of a cybersecurity strategy or its misalignment with the business's objectives.

Most of the time, cyber risks themselves are unclear because organizations lack the data required to understand the frequency of the various cyber-attacks that exist, the severity of these attacks, and how the attacks leverage vulnerable technologies and third-party service providers that are unique to an organization's Internet presence. Cyber risk quantification empowers organizations to quickly answer the following questions:

▪ Where should we spend our next dollar on our cyber strategy?
▪ Why should we spend it, and how does it enable our business?
▪ What is the financial impact of the cyber risks that are we likely to encounter?

As a member of the BOD or a C-LE, you should know the cyber risks and the impact that a compromise or outage of IT systems could have on business operations in financial terms. Most organizations are still seeking to define this risk in qualitative terms (opinion-based terms) and are finding it challenging to map the information into dollar values that any BOD member or C-LE can comprehend. The *value-at-risk* (VaR) technique is one method for measuring cyber risk. The *cyber value-at-risk* (CVaR) method was reviewed at the World Economic Forum conference in 2015 and was declared a credible means of quantifying cyber risk.[1]

THE VALUE PROPOSITION OF CYBER VAR

Organizations are rethinking how they measure and communicate their cybersecurity metrics. The financial measurement of cyber risk is gaining traction. Why? There are several reasons:

▪ Cyber risk quantification enables security and business discussions to occur in a language that everyone understands.

▨ Quantifying cyber risk in monetary terms allows businesses to assess the cyber risk of various efforts. Executives may weigh the potential cost of cyber risk events against the value of revenue, customer, and market share growth targets.

When the most senior cybersecurity executive, in most instances the CISO, talks with the BOD and the CEO about cybersecurity and cyber risk reduction initiatives, cyber risk management investment decisions become easier. They are easier when the executives understand what's at stake. As a result:

▨ Critical risks are prioritized for mitigation or investment across numerous groups, subsidiaries, and business units.
▨ Business growth and risk-mitigation objectives are aligned with financially quantifiable cyber risk and ROI data.
▨ The company learns how to accept, transfer, or mitigate cyber risk by integrating cyber risk management into enterprise risk management (ERM) and governance, risk, and compliance (GRC) responsibilities.
▨ The company establishes a cyber risk management plan that prioritizes risk reduction, transfer, and retention responses based on risk appetite.
▨ The company improves its capacity to include cyber risk management in the enterprise risk management program.
▨ The company builds cybersecurity metrics that are tailored to the requirements of C-level executives and members of the BOD.
▨ There is a focus on providing a justifiable rationale for cyber risk management investments.
▨ The cyber risk strategy is spread throughout the organization's core business operations to determine risk-transfer initiatives.

There is an urgent need for a change of mindset. When executives make a cyber risk management investment decision based on a qualitative assessment, rather than a quantitative one, there is a high likelihood that the most critical assets will be identified based on opinion, not on facts. Such a decision is much more likely to be misguided, resulting in cyber value risk that will not enable the business to achieve its objectives when under attack. If a successful cyber-attack compromises an organization's "crown jewels," it will bring the business operations to a halt or severely cripple them. That means any existing cybersecurity strategy is deficient if it is not accurately aligned to business goals and objectives which will easily map to these most valuable assets. Incorporating the cyber risk management of valuable assets is imperative for any organization to determine the quantitative value and financial impact of any cyber-attack that materializes. Let's reflect on a case study below.

CASE STUDY: THE COLONIAL PIPELINE CYBER-ATTACK

In May 2021, a cyber incident occurred in which the IT system controlling one of the largest petroleum pipelines in the United States was breached. After a ransomware attack, the Colonial Pipeline shut down its massive oil pipeline and took some of its systems offline. The Colonial Pipeline attack is one of the most significant cyber-attacks on an American energy grid in history.

The Colonial Pipeline Corporation stated on May 7 that it had been the target of a "cybersecurity assault" that "involves ransomware," prompting the company to shut down critical infrastructure and the pipeline. Colonial admitted to paying $4.4 million in bitcoin (which is now worth significantly less, although they retrieved 64 bitcoins, which are now worth only $2.3 million).

Ransomware attacks use malware to lock companies out of their systems until they pay the ransom. Ransomware attacks have surged in the past few years and cost companies billions of dollars just in ransoms paid, not counting those not reported or any associated costs of having systems offline. Ransomware attacks have targeted everything from private businesses to governments to hospitals and healthcare systems. Healthcare systems are particularly desirable targets, given how urgent it is to get their systems back up as soon as possible. According to a cybersecurity specialist who reacted to this incident, the breach that brought down the nation's main gasoline pipeline and caused shortages throughout the East Coast was the consequence of a single hacked password.

One way to look at this is that the cyber-attack illustrates how cyber risks materialize when the cyber risk management investments are misplaced and misaligned. As discussed in the previous chapter on cybersecurity strategy, in foresight a robust cybersecurity strategy is critical for business operations to protect themselves against cyber risks and mitigate potential data breaches and other cyber threats to critical infrastructure and critical data. In hindsight, the Biden administration responded after the incident by invoking the critical infrastructure order.

EXECUTIVE'S GUIDE TO CYBER RISK MANAGEMENT

We have already defined what exactly is risk management in the previous chapter. According to the Factor Analysis of Information Risk (FAIR), "Risk management is the process of achieving and maintaining an acceptable level of exposure to loss, within the context of an organization's objectives and constraints."[2]

In any business, there are many cyber risks that result in losing consumer or customer data, compromising critical infrastructure, and having trade secrets become public knowledge. For cost- and resource-effective cyber risk management, organizations need as the first step to start prioritizing or focusing on the cyber risks to their most valuable assets: the "crown jewels," critical data, and infrastructure. Crown jewels will vary from one organization to the next. The Cambridge dictionary defines a crown jewel as:[3]

The most important or valuable part of something, especially the product or part of a company, etc. that makes the most money.

As the case study earlier in the chapter shows, a cyber-attack resulting from a single hacked password resulted in access to the critical infrastructure on Colonial Pipeline, causing the company to shut down its pipeline system. In response to this cyber-attack, the Biden administration should start looking at additional actions by revisiting its cybersecurity strategy, focusing on critical infrastructure. A value-centric approach to cybersecurity investments is crucial to prevent, defend against, and minimize the impact of these cyber-attacks by malicious actors within the organization and minimize any effects that may have widespread implications for or even cause devastation to the global economy.

Cyber risks vary from one organization to another. This leads to several questions for every organization:

- What will bring the business to its knees when the organization is subjected to a cyber-attack?
- Will someone in the organization mishandle or steal critical data or misconfigure critical infrastructure? How? When?
- How significant will the impact be?
- What can we, as BOD members and executives, do to address all these cyber risks?

The outcome-driven approach to answering the above questions is practical cyber risk management, which is based on facts and numbers. Then a cost- and resources-effective cyber risk management will increase the chances that an organization will achieve its goals and have more opportunities for success. When deployed well, cyber risk management techniques can answer questions such as these:

▪ Where is the organization most vulnerable?
▪ What are the organization's critical infrastructure and information assets?
▪ How should the organization spend the next dollar to get the most significant value from cyber risk management?

Most risk management systems follow a standard process:

1. Assets, threats, and vulnerabilities are identified.
2. Cyber risks are assessed.
3. Risks are prioritized based on potential harm.
4. Risks are treated.

A risk appetite statement expresses the attitude of the BOD and C-LEs toward risk in qualitative or quantitative terms. Most organizations use qualitative expressions of risk appetite that commonly include risk-neutral, risk-averse, and risk-seeking. We typically link qualitative risk appetite statements to operational and financial performance measures. Let's differentiate the two cyber risk management approaches.

▪ The quantitative approach focuses on the likelihood of a threat occurring and the impact on the business. Risks are often classified on a scale that assesses their likelihood (for example, low, medium, high), and the scale also ranks them depending on the source of the risk or its impact on the business. The experiences of subject matter experts serve as the foundation for qualitative risk assessments.
▪ The quantitative approach would have currency numbers for all cyber risk levels, potential loss, and cost of mitigation, which efficiently empowers risk prioritization. The cyber value precept facilitates effective and unambiguous risk-related discussions and informed decisions. This enhances the accuracy of risk evaluations, since they are based on data points rather than relative scales based on the personal experiences of subject matter experts. Effectively, the quantitative approach positions the BOD and

C-LEs to recognize, analyze, and prioritize how to make adequate investments to avoid potential cyber threats to business-critical infrastructure and data. Adopting a quantitative approach, articulated in financial terms of the probable outcomes of attaining specific business objectives, helps to clarify decision making when there is ambiguity and, last but not least, develops realistic and achievable cost/schedule/scope targets. FAIR is the recommended methodology to adopt for the quantitative approach. If an organization wants to start using this approach, it should refer to Jack Jones, *Measuring and Managing Information Risk: A FAIR Approach* (ISBN-13:978-0124202313; ISBN-10: 0124202314).

The purpose of cyber risk management, particularly enterprise risk management, is to empower leadership and the whole organization with the information needed to make business decisions based on an executive-approved risk appetite statement. Risk appetite guides the risk owners to determine the proper response strategy. All cyber risks will need a designated risk owner who ensures that someone in the organization is accountable for the risk. In the absence of that one person or a group charged with managing cyber risk, by default the entire organization will own the risk, making it highly likely that the cyber risk will fall through the cracks (because no one will do anything).

One key point is that the risk owner only provides risk treatment or the risk response strategy: in most cases, business for critical data or IT for critical infrastructure or technology. There are four risk treatment options. The acronym ACAT is used to remember them:

- ▧ **Avoid**: eliminate the threat to protect the assets from the impact of the cyber risk. For example, the organization can stop or avoid doing something that increases its cyber risk.
- ▧ **Control (Mitigate)**: act to reduce the impact of the risk or the probability of its occurrence. An example is that the organization can control the cyber risk by implementing procedures or measures to mitigate it.
- ▧ **Accept**: recognize the risk but take no action unless the risk happens. Documenting the cyber risk and setting money aside if it unfolds is one example of this. If the cost of risk reduction outweighs the asset's cost, the business can tolerate the risk.
- ▧ **Transfer**: shift the impact of the threat to a third party, together with ownership of the response. For example, the organization can transfer the risk by buying cyber insurance.

Risk response strategy evolves in response to changing business conditions, so continuous monitoring of cyber threats and the broader environment is critical.

 ## EXECUTIVE'S GUIDE TO FAIR CYBER VALUE-AT-RISK

While still considering the value proposition of cyber value outlined earlier, this book recommends that the BOD and C-LEs of organizations start their journey of cyber-risk quantification by adopting the international framework for cyber-risk quantification called FAIR (Factor Analysis of Information Risk).

The following is a summary of FAIR by Jack Jones, author of the FAIR standard and chairman of the FAIR Institute:

FAIR was developed to enable organization executives to understand and make well-informed decisions about cybersecurity. At its core, FAIR is simply a clear and concise decomposition of the factors that drive the frequency and magnitude of loss. This decomposition not only identifies the key factors that drive risk but also their relationships to one another. This, in turn, enables the application of well-established quantitative methods (e.g., Monte Carlo functions, calibrated estimation, etc.) to measure loss exposure as well as the reduction of loss exposure from improving controls.

An example of how this can improve decision making comes from an organization that had just undergone a cybersecurity audit. The auditors had labeled two of the audit findings as "high risk," which would have demanded immediate and costly remediation efforts. However, after a FAIR analysis, it was discovered that one of those findings did not represent significant loss exposure to the organization. In fact, it represented an order of magnitude lower exposure than would be required to be considered "high risk." The rigor and quantitative clarity provided by the FAIR analysis enabled the organization to avoid applying resources to a problem that didn't warrant immediate attention. Instead, those resources could be applied to other organization imperatives, such as growth or operational cost reduction.

Unfortunately, in the absence of an analytic approach like FAIR, organizations are unable to reliably identify and focus on the risks that matter most, or the risk reduction solutions that are most cost-effective. The result is wasted resources and chronic exposure to levels of risk that threaten an organization's ability to achieve its objectives.[4]

As you can see, it's critical that you take an analytical, quantitative approach to risk assessment. Any other (less scientifically stringent) approach can lead to misguided effort and potentially great loss.

 NEXT STEPS

Once a solid value-centric approach has been identified and the best approach chosen, it doesn't mean the organization is secure or that cyber-risk management is now operational. A few questions remain to be answered. Let's look at those questions now.

Where to Start to with Quantitative Risk Management?

The BOD must place the same value-focused emphasis on cybersecurity that it does on other business-related challenges, such as go-to-market, human resources, and cash flow. It all starts with the BOD and C-LEs, who should make available adequate financial resources to enable the people mandated to implement cybersecurity functions to adopt the cyber value precept. Then how will the BOD and C-LEs be able to quickly weigh the potential financial losses against the costs of managing cyber hazards? The FAIR methodology is a good starting point.

Like any business risk, in most organizations the cybersecurity function, would be part of the governance, risk, and compliance (GRC) sector. The cybersecurity experts need to empower the BOD and C-LEs by reporting cyber risks in monetary terms rather than explaining technological complexities. In most businesses, the GRC function is mandated to have effective cyber risk management that oversees cyber-risk quantification. As with other critical business problems, GRC can also enlist the assistance of experienced cyber-risk quantification specialists.

How Do You Measure the Efficiency of Cyber Risk Mitigation Controls?

Since areas for attack are proliferating and the internal and external threat landscape is changing rapidly, organizations must continuously undertake cybersecurity assessments. Executives must ensure that the business tests its cybersecurity controls using simulations of actual cyber-attacks. These simulations must justify whether the cybersecurity investment enabled the organization to resist new and evolving threat scenarios and attack vectors and whether the cyber-risk analysis provided assurance that the business operations were minimally impacted by a significant cyber-attack. Executives always prioritize one strategy over another. Leaders often seek data to inform their choices and make their decisions. The same is true with cyber risk; correct data makes decision-making easy.

However, these cyber risks that are difficult to quantify frequently set the discourse in making cyber risk management investments. The next course of action is to measure cyber risks quantitatively. Cyber VaR—implemented well—will enable an organization to manage cyber risks while meeting the goals of its cybersecurity strategy. Some objectives include:

▒ Achieving customer expectations
▒ Being resilient to cyber-attacks and cyber failures
▒ Complying with laws and regulations
▒ Driving ideas for the next innovations in a secure way
▒ Achieving business growth and sustainability

Start-Ups and Small- and Medium-Sized Businesses (SMBs)

Most start-ups and small- and medium-sized businesses (SMBs) would not have the financial resources to adopt the quantitative approach or fully-fleshed-out GRC function. The initial step is to articulate clearly the risk appetite statement and the organization's risk tolerance. This will enable the start-up or SMB to decide the cyber risk management approach to adopt that would allow the founders and executive team to visualize a complete picture of the organizational cyber risk level. Adopting a risk management framework helps business leaders evaluate the potential risks and decide what responses to handle the cyber risks and crises are within the organization's risk appetite. The ISO 31000 framework would be a good starting point to identify risks by evaluating the information/data obtained. Cyber risk management using the qualitative approach still enables the decision-making process by involving consideration of political, social, economic, people, and technology factors with relevant risk assessments related to a potential hazard. Even in today's risk management, qualitative approaches are still used to manage and minimize the uncertainty and threats realization to the organizations. A qualitative approach remains relevant and applicable only if effectively deployed. As the organizations grow, they can start having a hybrid model that is both semi-qualitative and semi-quantitative.

Start-up founders and SMB business executives can refer to Appendix B for a high-level overview of ISO 31000.

Cyber risk management is a practice that any organization might have deployed, but unless critically evaluated, it might remain ineffective. There are many risk management standards or frameworks, including ISO 31000 from the International Organization for Standardization (ISO; see www.iso.org/iso-31000-risk-management.html), FAIR (Factor Analysis of Information Risk; see www.fairinstitute.org), and NIST Special Publication 800-30 (see https://csrc.nist.gov/publications/detail/sp/800-30/rev-1/final).

 ## SUMMARY

Cyber value is a core principle that all executives need to understand, as this understanding will make it easier to align their cybersecurity strategy with other business principles. Cyber value enables the adequate representation of cyber risk and the formulation of a holistic cyber risk management strategy that incorporates risk mitigation, risk transfer, and risk retention. Implementing cyber risk management in quantifiable terms helps organizations analyze and manage their cyber risk by defining it in commercial terms.

In summary, cyber value makes it easy for all executives to understand how cyber risk affects future revenue, profits, and other measurements of financial performance. Cyber value is a subset of a robust cybersecurity strategy that will require financial support from the organization, which is justifiable since it will align executives to every cybersecurity investment affecting the business. When the organization's BOD, C-Les, and founders have effective cyber risk management, it gives them the confidence to take the subsequent strategic business risk by leveraging innovation-powered growth for sustainability. The next step is a precept that focuses on industry-specific and regulatory compliance risks.

 ## NOTES

1. https://www3.weforum.org/docs/WEFUSA_QuantificationofCyberThreats_Report2015.pdf
2. https://www.fairinstitute.org/
3. https://dictionary.cambridge.org/dictionary/english/crown-jewel
4. Courtesy of Jack Jones, award-winning CISO, author of the FAIR standard, and chairman of the FAIR Institute

CHAPTER THREE

Cyber Compliance

The Compliance-Centric Approach

The knock-on effect of a data breach can be devastating for a company. When customers start taking their business—and their money—elsewhere, that can be a real body blow.

—Christopher Graham[1]

 INTRODUCTION

The first chapter established a cybersecurity strategy, and the second outlined how organizations can adopt the cyber value precept to align cyber risk management in business terms (dollars). This chapter focuses on how the BOD and C-LEs can ascertain cyber compliance with the established rules, regulations, laws, and policies. Noncompliance can bring about a fatally defective state of affairs for any organization. Once the precepts in previous chapters have been adopted, they ensure proactive cybersecurity and ensure that cyber risk management controls are implemented for critical assets; having a precept for compliance with laws, regulatory, privacy, industry-specific standard matures the organization's cybersecurity posture to the next level. The BOD and C-LEs must understand the need to innovate and protect the critical data of their customers, employees, and business partners, a task that is increasingly challenging in this era of cyber-attacks. Achieving cyber compliance outcomes does not happen by chance. It requires a thoughtful, focused approach. Cyber compliance demands an interdisciplinary systems-engineering approach because it is diverse.

Cyber compliance remains imperative for the BOD and C-LEs because it demonstrates the ability to secure and protect digital data, both the business's and customers' data, which yields a competitive advantage. Cyber compliance is a compliance-centric approach that enables executives to recognize, analyze, and address industry-specific and regulatory compliance cyber risk, which is critical for effective cyber risk management.

To begin with, executives of an organization need to be mindful of the cyber compliance requirements within their specific jurisdiction and industry. It is of paramount importance that all business executives strive to minimize the cyber risks related to noncompliance, for a lack of compliance has adverse effects on their reputation at large, not to mention the damage it can do to the organization. Executives can take one of two approaches to cyber compliance requirements:

▪ Board members and business executives can elect not to have a vested interest in any topics related to cyber compliance topics and rely on the legal team or the cybersecurity team to handle it all. The chances are that stakeholders will suffer discomfort or damage from the legal ramifications of a cyber-attack caused by misalignment. That is called hindsight.

▪ Board members and business executives can seek to comprehend the cyber compliance regulations and invest time and communication to ensure adequate financial support for both the cybersecurity and legal counsel functions. This approach is best described as having foresight.

As much as the cybersecurity strategy is well outlined or shared with the board members and business executives, cyber compliance is an additional precept that articulates which laws, regulations, and requirements apply to the organization. Most organizations have a compliance program that specifies rules, standards, and controls assurance. Policies and standards will never cover all conceivable cyber risk scenarios, nor do they imply that all cyber risk potential losses are covered. There are also compliance frameworks that are emerging from external requirements.

Executives are the most significant members of an organization because they can cause the most reputational damage. They must uphold compliance, accountability, and ethical behavior. If a leader's tone lacks compliance integrity, they will convey the wrong message to employees, consumers, customers, and partners. The tone at the top establishes the organization's guiding values and ethical compliance atmosphere. Creating and maintaining the right tone at the top is the foundation of a strong compliance culture. Consumers, customers, and business partners evaluate the credibility of business executives based in part on their ability to uphold compliance and maintain integrity.

CYBER COMPLIANCE

We can then define cyber compliance as a collection of rules that ensures a system of governance, risk mitigation, and cybersecurity controls that operate in accordance with guidelines. We may draw this ruleset from a published specification set by a legislative, regulatory, or self-regulatory agency.

According to Francesca Sales, compliance risk is defined as follows:

> Compliance risk is an organization's potential exposure to legal penalties, financial forfeiture, and material loss, resulting from its failure to act in accordance with industry laws and regulations, internal policies or prescribed best practices. Compliance risk is also known as integrity risk. Organizations of all types and sizes are exposed to compliance risk, whether they are public or private entities, for-profit or non-profit, state, or federal. An organization's failure to comply with applicable laws and regulations can affect its revenue, which can lead to loss of reputation.[2]

Cyber compliance can also include adherence to various controls (often imposed by a regulatory body, legislation, or industry association) to preserve the confidentiality, integrity, and availability of data. The next section considers a case study where lack of cyber compliance had long-lasting negative effects.

THE VALUE PROPOSITION OF CYBER COMPLIANCE

There has been increased attention by regulators and authorities on cyber compliance. Cyber compliance is critical to reducing the burden, the risk of penalties, and the risk of damage to an organization's reputation. When compliance risks are ignored or left unabated, this can cause an irretrievable collapse of an organization's reputation, assets, and trustworthiness. The inevitable damage from noncompliance often outweighs any success of the organization.

The absence of a compliance-centric or a compliance-by-design approach is evidence that the organization doesn't comply with laws, regulations, or industry standards. Cyber compliance will only ensure that the business will remain viable and sustainable for the foreseeable future as long the cyber compliance is clearly articulated and understood.

Clearly articulated cyber compliance builds trusted partnerships with any company already engaged or planning to partner with your organization. Cyber compliance validates business integrity. Business integrity reinforces trust relationships with consumers, customers, and business partners. It also ensures that the organization prioritizes integrity as one of its values, which strengthens the industry and improves economic security.

Companies with strong ethical management teams enhance their ability to attract investors, customers, and talented professionals. Such businesses remain viable and sustainable into the foreseeable future if cyber compliance is continuously articulated and maintained. Compliance is directly related to trust. People trust the brand, product, company, or business and voluntarily defer to the decisions of organizations that maintain compliance. Trust is earned when the board and business executive insist that employees at every level understand the importance of keeping their word and living up to regulatory laws and company compliance requirements. Externally, partners, consumers, and customers will always want to know that they can depend on the organization.

Cybersecurity breaches are not limited to financial losses but also adversely affect an organization's reputation, which might harm a business's ability to keep its consumers. Cyber compliance is the key to trust, growth, and profitability. Cyber compliance also establishes a preliminary level of trust with an organization's employees, customers, consumers, and third parties, which boosts its business growth.

 ## CASE STUDY

The GDPR (General Data Protection Regulation) is a collection of data privacy legislation enacted by the EU in 2018 to "harmonize data privacy laws across

Europe."[3] The GDPR applies to EU member states and the European Economic Area (EEA) and addresses the security issues surrounding transferring personal data beyond the EU and EEA. It implies that GDPR obligations apply to any entity that gathers data on or targets citizens in the EU, regardless of where the business or organization is located.

The GDPR's principal purpose is to offer consumers more control over their personal data while also simplifying the legal environment for foreign enterprises by consolidating legislation throughout the EU. The GDPR includes provisions for personal data protection, data minimization, and information security. It embodies the EU legislators' commitment to harmonize data protection policies and regulations across the EEU by imposing hefty fines on any violations.

According to the Data Privacy Manager blog (https://dataprivacy manager.net), the Hamburg Commissioner for Data Protection and Freedom of Information (BfDI) issued a €35,3 (or $41.5) million fine to the Swedish retail conglomerate Hennes & Mauritz (H&M) for its violation of the GDPR regulations.[4]

Due to a technical error, the data on the company's network drive was accessible to everyone in the company for a few hours. The press picked up the news, making the commissioner aware of the violation. The case is interesting because the company collected sensitive personal data about their employees through whispering campaigns, gossip, and other sources to create profiles of employees and used that data during the employment process.

As you can see, violating cyber compliance requirements can result in significant financial loss.

Poor compliance always results in punitive consequences. On the other hand, effective compliance may lower liabilities, boost operational efficiency, and enhance the customer experience.

 ## EXECUTIVE'S GUIDE TO CYBER COMPLIANCE

Compliance requirements vary significantly by jurisdiction, making it difficult to codify regulations at the global level. This raises many questions as organizations grapple with the implications of cyber compliance. We answer two of these questions in this section.

Which compliance requirements apply to this organization?

Whether legislative or regulatory, cyber compliance obligations heavily depend on the kind of data the business stores and processes, the industry it is in, the regulatory bodies for that industry, and the geographic boundaries within which the organization operates.

How can the executives handle cyber compliance and stay in control in such a complex compliance landscape?

The overflow of compliance requirements introduces new challenges, not limited to conflicting and challenging policies and to increased operational costs and disparate processes. Boards and business executives are encouraged to increase their focus and attention on cyber compliance risk by receiving regular updates that enable monitoring and maintaining control of the cyber compliance obligations of the organization.

One of the many responsibilities of an organization's executives is to ensure that the organization meets all cyber compliance requirements. They also must ensure that those entrusted with monitoring all cyber compliance requirements constantly guard against any form of malpractice that could endanger the swift flow of business. Executives should regularly seek evidence of compliance with all the policies, standards, laws, and regulations applicable to the organization.

Every business executive trusts that all employees will act in the business's best interest to achieve its objectives, but this also needs to be validated. All these actions require constant validation. Validation and verification require the executives to comprehend the cyber compliance requirements applicable to the business. This knowledge is essentially a recipe for ease in cyber investment decision making and for articulating reports. A better understanding of the cyber risks will ease the discussion in the board and management meetings and empower executives to formulate questions for senior cybersecurity executives, enabling better decision making. A question as simple as, "How are we doing from a cyber compliance perspective?" can spur on a value-added discussion.

In most cases, the topic of cyber compliance is avoided and left for others to manage and maintain. Many executives develop an interest in a compliance-centric approach only after a hefty fine is levied. Foresight about cyber compliance can prevent such issues from cropping up.

CYBER COMPLIANCE CLASSIFICATIONS

Globally, the complexity of cyber compliance laws, regulations, and standards have led to chaos and stifled businesses. The differing requirements of these laws make it hard to articulate what to do or not do. With the emergence of new cyber-attacks and efforts by the public or private sector to coordinate policies, the chaos is unlikely to abate soon. In response to the growth of cyber threats, regulators have issued frameworks, guidelines, and standards to ensure that organizations implement cybersecurity processes and control measures in healthcare, financial services, and government departments to minimize the impact of cyber risks.

The regulations and industry standards are designed to protect critical information and infrastructure and force organizations to reduce cyber risks. We can classify how compliance requirements differ from one organization to another, but most requirements fall under the following categories:

- **Specific to laws, regulations, and legislation:** Privacy laws are considered within the consumer industry. Privacy laws that have been most prevalent lately include the General Data Protection Regulation (GDPR) of the European Union, which regulates the data protection and privacy of citizens of the European Union. GDPR applies to any company doing business in the European Union or handling the data of any citizen of the European Union. Similar privacy laws have been passed elsewhere, such as the California Consumer Privacy Act (CCPA).
- **Government-specific:** US President Joe Biden recently issued an executive order (EO) to improve the nation's cybersecurity. The EO is an example of a government-specific compliance requirement mandating that organizations follow certain policies or guidance, timelines, and minimum-security requirements and standards.
- **Industry-specific:** Industry-specific policies and procedures determine how information should be protected. Consider these two examples:
  - **Health Sector: Health Insurance Portability and Accountability Act (HIPAA).** In the US, HIPAA mandates that healthcare institutions, insurers, and third-party service providers maintain measures for safeguarding and preserving patient data, as well as undertake risk assessments to identify and mitigate emerging threats. The act applies to any organization that handles healthcare data; that includes, but is not limited to, doctor's offices, hospitals, insurance companies, business associates, and employers.
  - **Financial Sector: PCI DSS.** The popular PCI DSS standards consist of 12 regulations aimed at decreasing fraud and securing customer credit card information. Any organization that handles credit card information should be aware of it.
- **Company/business-specific:** In the absence of complete alignment with regulatory, legislative, or industry guidelines, which is very unlikely, a company's board and executives should mandate the ethics and level of compliance that define company-specific compliance requirements.

Compliance in collaboration with cyber teams and legal counsel can then determine company-specific policies and procedures to maintain a level of cyber compliance. There can be additions to government and industry-specific cyber compliance requirements.

▪ **Information security best practice framework–specific:** The National Institute of Standards and Technology (NIST) is an example of a voluntary framework that any organization can implement to reduce its overall risk.

Executives are not expected to know everything there is about cyber compliance. The first step of this process is to know which regulations, laws, and acts apply to your organization. After this first step, the organization should develop a business strategy that works within the boundaries of the regulations, laws, acts, policies, and standards. This level of understanding helps the organization encourage a cyber compliance culture and enforce cyber risk management.

NEXT STEPS AND REFLECTION

Compliance applies to all organizations irrespective of size. Transitioning to a collaborative functional model based on governance, risk, and compliance (GRC) principles causes organizations to connect many departments and job responsibilities digitally. Only then can GRC procedures link the relevant information at the right moment, allowing stakeholders to take the optimal action. There are several techniques, and they must be adaptable enough to adjust swiftly to changing conditions established by regulators and corporate priorities. After all, regulators have enormous power over compliance operations, but institutions reap significant benefits from spreading compliance processes and procedures across many departments.

Compliance by Design: Compliance by design is taking a methodical approach to incorporating regulatory requirements. Compliance by design method in growing business models, particularly in a fast-changing technology context, is a more dynamic and adaptive approach to regulatory compliance with a long-term emphasis. Regulatory bodies are increasingly under political pressure to guarantee that innovation leads to competitive market outcomes that benefit customers. This pressure may cause uncertainty for compliance stress testing, which implies becoming more inventive. A compliance-centric strategy aids in the assessment and mitigation of potential regulatory issues.

For privacy-specific issues, it would be a good start to adopt the privacy-by-design methodology.

Privacy by Design: Privacy by Design is a framework for proactively incorporating privacy into the design and operation of information technology systems, networked infrastructure, and business activities. Privacy by design entails incorporating privacy into the design, operation, and administration of a system, business process, or design specification; it is founded on the seven foundational principles developed initially by Ann Cavoukian in 1995.

1. Proactive not reactive; preventive, not remedial
2. Privacy as the default setting
3. Privacy embedded into the design
4. Full functionality—positive-sum, not zero-sum
5. End-to-end security—complete lifecycle protection
6. Visibility and transparency—keep it open
7. Respect for user privacy—keep it user-centric

Appendix C has further information on privacy by design and the seven foundational principles, with implementation and mapping of fair information principles by Ann Cavoukian, PhD. There is already comprehensive privacy management software that can help growing businesses operationalize and simplify compliance and privacy by design.

 ## SUMMARY

Cyber compliance management is an ongoing, cyclical endeavor. This is because the cyber risk landscape is constantly changing; therefore, the comprehensive list of related regulatory, governmental, and industry requirements is also continuously evolving.

A challenge every organization faces is that as these extensive requirements vary, organizations must map the requirements to existing internal organizational policies to identify the gaps in their cyber compliance risk posture and update them. Regulations, laws, and government-wide policies will always create requirements and must be folded into more comprehensive cyber risk management approaches as priorities or threat environments change within organizations. Most organizations mandate cybersecurity executives (in most cases, CISOs) to explain the applicability of specific industry laws, regulations, and compliance requirements in business operations and evaluate any changes required by the organization to meet its objective with minimum compliance-related risks. In order for the CISO to be able to provide that assurance, the executives need to make adequate investments in cyber compliance risk management.

Most organizations do not have a compliance-centric approach in place. Also, most businesses are far too small to justify hiring a CISO to oversee cybersecurity and cyber compliance. In these cases, another approach to consider is consulting with a cybersecurity firm or an attorney specializing in cyber law to determine what compliance standards may apply to the organization and how to manage compliance risk throughout the organization's operations.

This chapter explained why the foundational knowledge and an understanding of cyber compliance enable executives to differentiate what regulatory, industry-specific, and best-practice requirements their organizations need to comply with. They must address these challenges, manage any cyber risk, and give cyber compliance the priority it deserves. This does not happen in a vacuum. This is accomplished by creating a compliance-focused approach as part of the organization's culture. As previously explained, when data under an organization's control is compromised, it causes major media waves. Data breaches occur in different ways and sizes. One of the most destructive is an unintentional data breach caused by an employee. The consequences of such data exposure may be tremendous for an organization, since not only is the loss of sensitive data embarrassing and detrimental to their reputation, but it can also have an influence on their compliance posture and result in significant fines. Developing a human-centric approach can help executives avoid becoming a cautionary tale. Let's see how it goes in the following chapter.

 NOTES

1. https://www.blue-pencil.ca/8-tweetable-cybersecurity-quotes-to-help-you-and-your-business-stay-safer/
2. Sales, F. (n.d.). "Compliance Risk." Retrieved from TechTarget: https://search compliance.techtarget.com/definition/compliance-risk?utm_campaign=20210817_ ERU+Transmission+for+08%2F17%2F2021+%28UserUniverse%3A+319 235%29&utm_medium=EM&utm_source=ERU&src=8099605&asrc=EM_ ERU_175993839&utm_content=eru-rd2-control
3. https://gdpr-info.eu/
4. https://dataprivacymanager.net/german-dpa-issued-e353-million-gdpr-fine-to-hm-for-violation-of-the-general-data-protection-regulation/

CHAPTER FOUR

Cyber Culture

The Human-Centric Approach

Organizational culture must be reinvented for the information age.

—Christiane Wuillamie, OBE, chief executive of PYXIS Culture Technologies Ltd

INTRODUCTION

In earlier chapters, we explored cybersecurity strategy, cyber value, and cyber compliance precepts for effective cyber risk management. This chapter focuses on one of the most fundamental precepts that intertwines all precepts concerning cyber risks—the human element. Even if the BOD and C-LEs understand all three tenets outlined in the previous chapters, this does not guarantee that the business is secure. Every cyber breach has a human thumbprint, which makes cyber risk everyone's issue in any organization. From the top to the bottom, everyone must be accountable for cyber risks.

Organizations will still be continually subjected to cyber-attacks despite establishing a cybersecurity strategy, adopting the cyber value precept, and being cyber compliant with laws and regulations. Malicious actors are exploiting or profiting from human mistakes that give attackers access to secured critical infrastructure and critical information. A cyber culture is a missing link for cybersecurity strategy to be more effective. Organizations must recognize that technology alone will not eliminate attackers. Organizations must begin harnessing human intelligence (judgment) as a critical component for success in today's cyber risk landscape. Without a human-centric approach, organizations will continue to lack the fundamental skills to defend against the most sophisticated attacks; they cannot rely on technology alone to solve what appear to be technological problems. One lament that resonates strongly in information security is that we're not doing enough to deal with cybersecurity's biggest, most persistent threat—human behavior. Human judgment is still required to bridge the gap between cybersecurity technology capabilities and cybersecurity strategy. We can acknowledge that human judgment isn't perfect and also that technology isn't sufficient to mitigate behavioral risks.

 ## WHAT IS CULTURE ANYWAY?

Most academics and business leaders equate culture with employee behavior. For a long time, culture has been defined as "the way we do things around here." Employee behavior is not the culture, but the outcome of a collection of policies, work practices, leadership, compensation, and organizational structure that have a direct influence on employee behavior. This organizational ecosystem is the culture, and employee behavior is the outcome.

A simple example: The compensation policies of large bonuses in investment banking have a strong influence that drives excessive risk-taking and sometimes leads to fraudulent behavior among traders. Even traffic police are influenced by a policy that pays them based on the number of tickets written, not the quality of the offenses cited. The organizational culture drives employee behavior.

Policies, work practices, and other organizational elements are established by the BOD and senior management. Therefore, the BOD and C-LEs must take the lead in building a cyber risk culture. Most organizations' culture is designed to meet established financial targets, customer satisfaction, and employee retention. Effective cyber risk culture is built and sustained through well-thought-out policies and work practices that drive cyber awareness and accountability in all employees.

While continuous cyber awareness messaging and training are important, the wrong policies and work practices can quickly negate good training. A manager who is rewarded for meeting cost or schedule targets at the expense of cybersecurity has a powerful impact on the behavior of employees and their attitudes toward cybersecurity and risk. In many organizations, business leaders have never invested interest in fully understanding how the culture's ecosystem impacts employee cyber behaviors. Executives often cultivate an organizational culture that minimizes the need for cyber risk management, which is only addressed by cybersecurity governance teams. A human-centric approach to mitigating cyber risk is as critical for any organization as addressing the human element in increasing market share or meeting financial targets. A cyber risk–aware culture will exist only when everyone jointly works toward one enterprise-wide cyber risk management strategy. This must start from the top down—with the executives and board members. If the BOD and C-LEs do not value the need for a cyber risk–aware culture, employees down the line will not value it either, sometimes with catastrophic consequences.

According to a study by IBM, an average of about 95% of cyber breaches are from human behavior (be it through negligence or malicious actions).[1] But the risk from an improper human-centric approach extends beyond the business user to the software developers, who may have designed an application that doesn't incorporate security by design. The root causes of these human behaviors and aspects of cyber risk culture contribute to the trajectory of cyber-attacks.

The phrase "humans are the weakest link" is now obsolete. Instead of humans being considered the weakest link in the security chain, the narrative must change to "humans are the first and last line of defense" in any organization.

Cyber risk–aware culture is imperative for organizations that still need to meet business goals and objectives and remain sustainable. The question for any executive to ask is, "Does my organization have a cyber risk–aware culture and strategy that efficiently manages the cyber risks of the employees and the customers?" Humans are critical to mitigating and minimizing cyber risks. It all comes down to a cyber culture being in the organization's DNA and thus passed down to its employees.

BUILDING A HUMAN-CENTRIC APPROACH TO RISK MANAGEMENT

As cyber-attacks proliferate globally, organizations have become more aware of the criticality of human cybersecurity. Practical cyber training has been the traditional approach and a single buffer against a crippling attack. But despite this awareness, organizations will still battle a disengaged and sometimes openly indifferent workforce, and issues have increased because of remote working during the pandemic.

It is a fair assumption that over 90% of successful cyber-attacks have an element of human interaction, making it imperative for organizations to evolve or enhance the human-element approach to cyber risk management. Malicious actors have consistently and successfully targeted humans with social engineering efforts to siphon sensitive corporate data and more.

Most firms provide extensive cybersecurity awareness training, yet it has little effect on behavior. A human-centric strategy must be ingrained in business culture to improve cyber risk mitigation. While cybersecurity training is essential for raising awareness, it is merely the first step in reducing cyber risk from a human-centric standpoint. The next step is to incorporate ongoing cybersecurity into the corporate culture. The next level of maturity in comprehensive human training occurs when an organization has a cyber culture (human-centric approach).

The human-centric approach varies from one organization to another. The human-centric strategy of companies developing applications accessible to customers or used by other organizations differs from that of an organization providing direct services to consumers. For the organization that develops applications, the BOD and C-LEs of that organization should develop a cyber risk–aware culture so that their products are cyber-secure. The organization that processes consumer data should have a cyber risk awareness culture about consumer data privacy laws. The sources of cyber vulnerabilities from a human element include, but are not limited to, the following:

- Viewing cybersecurity as a technology issue alone.
- Company policies that inadvertently drive risky behaviors.
- Absence of an organizational cyber risk–aware culture.
- Absence of a clear leadership stance on cyber risks.
- A lack of employee awareness of and personal responsibility for cyber risk.
- A weak organizational process for addressing cyber risks; for example, employees being able to detect spear-phishing emails.

▪ Weak cyber risk mitigation procedures to follow, resulting in behaviors that increase the risk to internal systems and processes.

Every organization, large or small, successful or unsuccessful, has a unique culture. Just as every individual has a unique personality, every company has a unique identity, a corporate culture. An organization's policies, history, hero stories, values, and customs create the culture. This culture contributes to the definition of an organization's work and the business atmosphere. The management philosophy, style, and behaviors are all drivers of the corporate culture.

A robust cyber risk–aware culture serves multiple functions. For starters, it guides employees' efforts and ensures everyone is working toward the same goals, minimizing cyber risks. Furthermore, company culture assists newcomers in learning accepted attitudes and behaviors. If financial success is the cornerstone of the culture, newcomers rapidly discover that profit and costs are more important than cybersecurity.

The Value Proposition of a Cyber Culture

Humans inside an organization are the favorite targets of advanced cyber-attacks by hostile actors. A human-centric culture that is risk-conscious cultivates an awareness among all employees that helps to protect the organization's critical information and infrastructure. A risk-aware culture is crucial to elevating an organization's overall cyber risk management maturity. When a cyber culture is embedded from top to bottom, the organization is significantly more hardened than it is from a simple training or awareness campaign approach. Risk-aware culture ensures that everyone in the organization understands and has the capabilities for cyber risk mitigation.

In my experience, most people's perceptions of cybersecurity were inversely connected to the frequency with which humans engaged in unsafe cybersecurity behaviors. This requires that any BOD member or C-LE for any organization, regardless of its size or complexity, regard the ability to instill solid cybersecurity behavior (cyber culture) as critical.

 CASE STUDIES: HUMAN ERROR INCIDENTS

One of most significant data breaches caused by human mistakes occurred in 2015, when an NHS (National Health Service) practice disclosed the email addresses (and consequently names) of over 800 HIV patients. The NHS in the United Kingdom sent an email message to HIV patients and inadvertently typed their email addresses into the "to" field rather than the "bcc" field, thus exposing their personal information to each other.[2] This is a classic example of a human knowledge error, since the employee understood the correct course of action but did not take adequate care to ensure that they were doing what they desired to undertake.

Another example is the Colonial Pipeline ransomware attack, which is discussed in detail in Chapter 2. It shut down gas supplies in six US states and impacted over a million customers for several days.[3] The attack cost the company upwards of 5 million dollars in ransom payments, not to mention the lost revenue and recovery costs. The successful attack came from a single compromised employee password.

In the last few years, ransomware has become a genuine threat for the average organization. Each night, there is news of malicious hackers and advanced cyber-attacks that successfully compromise public and private organizations. Ransomware is one threat that has a 95% human element to it. Business leaders should become prepared, because the disruptions to business operations will worsen for the foreseeable future. The 2021 assaults were immensely effective and profitable, making a nasty trend simple to forecast. Ransomware attacks will worsen before improving. The techniques and goals of malicious actors are developing, which will certainly result in a harsher series of attacks on organizations. Cybercriminals have become more strategic in their ransomware assaults to maximize the potential damage to and payout from an organization.

Let's take a deep dive into the top ransomware attack vectors with human-element at a high level; these should remain relevant for the foreseeable future.

1. Email phishing: The vast majority of ransomware is distributed through email phishing campaigns. In these, attackers use legitimate-looking emails to deceive a person into visiting a malicious URL or opening an attachment containing malware. The URL takes the target to a rogue website, from which ransomware is downloaded. Hackers employ standard file types such as Word, PDF, Excel, and ZIP files to make attachments less suspicious. When the attachment is opened, the ransomware immediately starts encrypting and storing files for the hacker. Knowledge (the human aspect) is vital for lowering the cyber risk from exposure to phishing. Users, for example, should be able to distinguish between genuine and counterfeit URLs. Manually typing links in the browser, lingering over URLs, and expanding shortened URLs can keep users from clicking on fraudulent

links. Examine the domain extension of any email with attachments to see if the sender's email address is valid. Also, only open files received from trusted sources.

2. Downloads: Malicious actors can also spread malware by exploiting weaknesses in the backend of reputable websites. They can use the attack vector to inject malware or redirect site users to web pages under their control. Exploit kits enable malicious actors to evaluate the device for flaws covertly; if any are found, ransomware is executed in the background while the user does nothing. So assume that a user goes to an infected website. The user then gets a ransom note telling them about the virus and demanding payment, but a human would not understand because the infection (download) is invisible to users.

3. Unapproved software: Using unlicensed software on your Windows, Mac, or Linux computer might potentially raise your vulnerability to ransomware assaults. This is because an unlicensed program does not get official fixes from the author. Attackers exploit flaws in such software and then repackage it for distribution on pirate networks. When users download the program, they believe they are obtaining the most recent application, game, or key generator for free. However, users will be prompted to pay a ransom when installing it. In addition to torrent networks, hackers may distribute ransomware via YouTube and bogus crack sites. Users can easily avoid ransomware outbreaks caused by illegal software by not downloading activation, key generators, and software cracks from torrent websites.

4. Removable media: Ransomware may infiltrate removable media devices such as USB flash drives and memory sticks. Hackers infect portable devices with malicious software and then wait for unwary people to attach them to their PCs. This is especially dangerous if the user's PC is connected to a business network, as the ransomware might infect the whole firm. Furthermore, if a system has been attacked through a removable media port, its locally installed cloud drives can get infected as well.

Although there is technology like advanced antivirus software that can detect and eliminate ransomware from removable devices or protect users' devices by avoiding plugging in USB devices and hard drives, the human remains the first line of defense. In each actor vector outlined above, the human can take the first action and not do a step that could compromise the company through being cyber risk–aware. Technology can significantly boost most cybersecurity lines, but it can't do much about the person sitting behind the computer. It all comes back to an organization's cyber culture.

Cyber culture will become a lifestyle in which humans learn to prevent, detect, and mitigate ransomware. The key is for users to learn how to identify potential red flags, which will help to stop these cyber-attacks before they wreak havoc on the organization's network.

As you can see, good, up-to-date cybersecurity technology is critical, but the organization must create a cyber culture as well.

 ## EXECUTIVE'S GUIDE TO CREATING A RISK-AWARE CULTURE

Organizations are shadows of their leaders . . . that's the good news and the bad news!

—John R. Childress, Chairman, PYXIS Culture Technologies Ltd

This brings us to the role of BOD members and C-LEs in transitioning from security awareness into cybersecurity culture. The essential critical cybersecurity mitigation control is a robust cybersecurity culture. It all starts from the top. A formal, top-down cyber culture statement should articulate high-level strategies and rules that align with the business's vision and mission, making them explicit and actionable, by using clear documentation, KPIs, and metrics. Besides having a cyber culture statement to mitigate cyber risk, a formalized cyber culture program also gives BOD members and C-LEs and CISOs a shared language to discuss cyber risk and security priorities.

How and where does a cyber risk–aware culture come into play? It results from an intentional choice by the board of directors and business executives to instill a cyber risk–aware culture in their organization. A risk-aware culture is built over time as part of a continuous and concentrated business strategy. To secure the future today, BOD members and C-LEs must build cyber risk management into the corporate culture. A culture of being cyber risk–aware not only helps protect the company but also enables innovation and growth.

As mentioned, leadership philosophy, style, and behavior influence corporate culture. Therefore, executive leadership must take decisive action to start developing the cyber risk culture they want for their organizations and then work to nourish that culture by communicating with everyone who works there.

A purposefully established human-centric approach is a commercial advantage that will serve any organization for years and will protect it from inroads by competitors. Employee development and the maintenance of a cyber risk culture begin with the hiring process, which includes carefully hand-picking people and being extremely explicit about expectations and business culture. Although leaders play an important role in developing others, the culture belongs to everyone in the organization. Culture is an organization's unspoken social order. It has a broad and long-lasting impact on attitudes and behaviors. The first and most important step leaders can take to maximize their worth while minimizing risks is to recognize how a cyber risk–aware culture works. When leaders and employees engage well, the latter will make a greater contribution to team communication and collaboration and will be encouraged to complete the mission and objectives provided by the organization, thereby improving cybersecurity.

For most organizations, the biggest bang for their security dollar in best reducing cybersecurity risk comes from educating their employees in how to spot and treat phishing scams.
—*Roger Grimes, author and data-driven defense evangelist, KnowBe4*

Cultural norms define what is encouraged, discouraged, accepted, or rejected within a group. When properly aligned with personal values, drives, and needs, culture can unleash tremendous amounts of energy toward a shared purpose and foster an organization's capacity to thrive. For better or worse, culture and leadership are inextricably linked. Founders and influential leaders often set new cultures in motion and imprint values and assumptions that persist for decades.

Over time, an organization's leaders can also shape culture through both conscious and unconscious actions (sometimes with unintended consequences). The best leaders are fully aware of the multiple cultures within which they are embedded, can sense when change is required, and can deftly influence the process. It is far more common for leaders seeking to build high-performing organizations to be confounded by culture. Indeed, many either let it go unmanaged or relegate it to the HR function, where it becomes a secondary concern for the business. They may lay out detailed thoughtful plans for strategy and execution, but because they don't understand culture's power and dynamics, their plans go off the rails.

Employees turn to company leadership to set standards for cyber risk management. If leaders want employees to adopt cyber risk–aware habits, they must convey that cyber risk management is a prominent concern. Leadership can accomplish this by identifying cyber dangers to their lines of business or product offerings. This entails collaboration to discuss cyber risk subjects, such as watching for emerging threats in the press, monitoring cyber risk metrics relevant to their business sector, and making cyber risk oversight a visible senior leadership concern.

> If you want to build security, avoid straining people, but rather teach them to be vigilant and long for customer trust and satisfaction. Cybersecurity culture can achieve more than prohibition posture.
>
> —*Stéphane Nappo*

For businesses to survive the changing world of cyber-attacks, corporate executives should undertake different duties, all of which rely on good communication and cyber risk–aware culture. The board of directors and executives:

- Must fully understand the culture and ecosystem that impact cyber risk management.
- Must inculcate the organization's culture into every employee. For example, information about an organization's cyber risk–aware culture is frequently included in training and orientation for newcomers. A concise and meaningful description of the organization's mission is also an effective communication tool.
- Must sustain and reward the risk-aware culture by acknowledging and supporting people who understand it and seek to promote it.

Having a culture that mitigates cyber risk is also socioeconomic responsibility. As organizations deploy a focused organization-wide risk culture, creating risk awareness among all employees and providing regular training on cyber risk contribute to making the world more cyber-secure. This makes it imperative that the BOD members and C-LEs have, at the minimum, a human-centric strategy to mitigate cyber risk. The BOD members and C-LEs should advocate creating a cyber risk culture as a future organizational component of a comprehensive cyber risk management approach. Business executives should continuously maintain and enhance it.

There is a misconception that the human element is limited only to end-users. Humans program and develop applications and software based on a business need or niche market opportunity. A cyber-secure development culture is a must for organizations that develop software or applications before being published or accessible to the world. Developing vulnerable software and applications is a human element that needs to be addressed from the top through a BOD and C-LE statement as part of the organization's vision of building a secure cyber world.

For businesses in the technology development industry, a cyber-secure culture (sometimes referred to as security by design) within the development team contributes to every aspect of cybersecurity strategy and cyber compliance (sometimes referred to as privacy-by-design). The cyber culture of security-by-design and privacy-by-design needs to be part of the organization's culture communicated by the BOD members and C-LEs. The BOD members and C-LEs should be cognizant that the security of the solutions developed by their company will only be as strong as the humans who will use them, often referred to as the "weakest link." Your company is responsible for the exploitation of any insecure web application developed by your organization or supplied to them, or the vulnerable software that the next person uses to accomplish their work. Application security is one line of protection against hackers that seek business-critical data. Web applications are one of the most common ways for attackers to compromise individuals and businesses. If an attacker exploits a vulnerability in an application, it provides potentially unlimited access. Malicious attackers that exploit a vulnerability or weakness in an application will also have access to all data the application has access to, regardless of the data security or network precautions that are in place. The BODs and C-LEs of organizations that are in the technology or application development sectors need to be cognizant that if they underinvest in cybersecurity, including failing to create a security-conscious cyber culture within the development teams, they will eventually be accountable, which will result in severe financial losses and a tarnished brand.

A strong cybersecurity culture is more than just an HR initiative or an action item for the IT department. Culture rules and culture has rules. It is up to leadership to build policies and work practices that support and sustain cybersecurity principles and awareness. Culture is either a security risk or enabler of awareness and best practices.
—*John R. Childress, Chairman, PYXIS Culture Technologies Ltd*

NEXT STEPS

Being cyber-aware is no longer a tech skill, it's a life skill.

—Anna Collard, SVP content strategy and evangelist at KnowBe4 Africa

Where to start from is always a conundrum for most organizations, including start-ups and SMBs. KnowBe4 is one of the world's largest integrated platforms for cybersecurity training that any organization can consult when it starts the journey toward a cyber risk–aware culture

The following is a summary by Anna Collard, SVP content strategy and evangelist at KnowBe4 Africa.

"C-level support is paramount in both driving a more secure culture and ensuring that everyone within the organization understands their role and responsibility in creating the desired state. Executive involvement goes beyond sponsorship or budget approval for an awareness project. When executives are the face of a campaign and lead by example, it becomes powerful, because people look at not only what their leaders are saying, but what they are doing.

It is also continuous; whereas some training has a beginning and an end, with security awareness training, there is no end. It's a bit like flossing, something that needs to be done consistently to show results.

"It is no secret that people learn differently; therefore, cookie-cutter content just will not do. Content needs to be provided in different versions and varieties that match your diverse learning population styles. Look for a provider that offers a user-friendly administrative interface, that allows you to assign, track and measure training efforts, and provides a wide variety of training content, including interactive modules, videos, games, posters and newsletters.

Simulated phishing tests are a standard training mechanism and should not be viewed as a 'got ya' exercise. Explain that this is a company-wide initiative to help teach and strengthen their ability to spot and report an attack. Advise that these are transferrable skills that they can share with their friends, family, and loved ones so that they can be more cyber safe in their personal lives.

Since we can't manage what we can't measure, quantifying the success of any security awareness program is crucial. When determining what metrics to focus on, it's best to select a few meaningful ones that can be quantified frequently to show the progress over periods. Although training completion rates and ongoing phishing click rates are important measurements to track, consider conducting an annual security culture assessment to measure the organization's maturity level over time and benchmark against others.

A Few Key Takeaways

- An effective security awareness training program should be both comprehensive and continuous . . . there is no end.
- Assign program to a communications specialist, not a security technical lead.
- Leverage engaging/interesting content, simulated attacks and insightful communications.
- Build a force of champions, advocates and executive support.
- Select a few critical metrics."

Security knowledge and values, beliefs, behaviors, norms, and pressures are actually a fundamental part of any larger organizational culture. And that means that we can't approach security in a compartmentalized way. We must make our approach to security culture part of our overall approach to organizational culture, or else things will feel out of step and create confusion at best or distrust and cynicism at worst. In the end, our quest for a security culture is really all about our quest for an organizational culture with security values woven through its fabric.

—*Perry Carpenter, chief evangelist and strategy officer, KnowBe4 Inc.*

Start-ups, Small and Medium-Sized Businesses (SMBs)

One prevalent fallacy concerning cyber-attacks is that they will never happen to start-ups and SMBs because they are so tiny. When a significant cyber incident occurs, small businesses and start-ups are the most impacted and are often forced them to scale back operations or close completely. The impact of cyber threats on start-ups and small businesses includes significant brand damage, which may hinder them from obtaining the next round of funding and keeping loyal consumers. Those that have kept normalcy have had to adapt or try to use new digital tools and platforms to interact with consumers, restore supply chains, and stay in touch with staff in the assault's aftermath. Developing a cyber risk–aware culture can enable start-ups and small businesses to remain compliant and secure in an increasingly unpredictable era of cyber-attacks.

Most news reports and media focus on large corporations, but many start-ups and SMBs are compromised regularly. Most small firms are unaware of their cyber risk, implying that there is no human-centric approach to their cyber risk management. Threat actors always view every organization, including start-ups and SMBs, as a potentially significant source of information for financial gain. Likely, many start-ups and small- and medium-sized businesses do not protect critical assets effectively because of a lack of scale in operations and experience. Start-ups may not have a sufficient security budget. However, they can still take actions with a lesser budget to reduce risks and develop a cybersecurity posture that protects the company and keeps critical assets secure. Always assume that cyber threats and vulnerabilities can originate within the organization. Most cyber threats have an element of human carelessness, which is the fundamental cause of a breach in 95% of cases. Organizations like KnowBe4 offer free tools and may provide an organization-specific strategy based on the financial capacity of the start-ups and SMBs that will allow them to begin a human-centric approach to cyber risk. Appendix D has more information on KnowBe4.

▓ SUMMARY

It all begins at the top, where the BOD members and C-LEs must embrace effective cyber risk management as a business enabler. The BOD and C-LEs must also continuously practice what they preach and hold everyone in the business accountable for maintaining an effective cyber risk management posture for the organization. They must help to embed cyber risk management into the culture through continuous communication and making it a priority. The BOD and C-LEs should be relentless at rewarding awareness exercises, positive reinforcement of good behavior, incentives for proactive actions, and engagement with industry leaders by reinforcing a cyber risk–aware culture that embraces critical cyber risk management for business growth. According to the ISO4, "A system is a combination of interacting elements organized to achieve one or more stated purpose. The interacting system elements that compose a system include hardware, software, data, humans, processes, procedures, facilities, materials, and naturally occurring entities."[4] Reflecting on the last four precepts, we have discussed most elements of a system regarding respective approaches to cyber risks. The next precept is the final one that sums up the five fundamental precepts that are key for BOD members, C-LEs, start-up founders, and SMB business executives to understand. Cyber resilience is the technology-centric approach.

NOTES

1. https://thehackernews.com/2021/02/why-human-error-is-1-cyber-security.html#:~:text='Human%20error%20was%20a%20major,in%2095%25%20of%20all%20breaches.&text=Mitigation%20of%20human%20error%20must,cyber%20business%20security%20in%202021
2. https://www.independent.co.uk/life-style/health-and-families/health-news/hiv-status-of-nearly-800-patients-accidentally-disclosed-by-nhs-clinic-10482655.html
3. https://www.bloomberg.com/news/articles/2021-06-04/hackers-breached-colonial-pipeline-using-compromised-password
4. International Organization for Standardization/International Electrotechnical Commission/Institute of Electrical and Electronics Engineers, ISO/IEC/IEEE 15288: 2015—Systems and software engineering—Systems life cycle processes (Geneva, Switzerland). https://www.iso.org/standard/63711.html

CHAPTER FIVE

Cyber Resilience

The Technology-Centric Approach

Cyber resilience is directly proportional to an organization's data governance maturity. If a company hasn't properly documented the value and business impact of their data with respect to their critical business processes, it is impossible for it to have cyber resiliency.

—Kevin L. Jackson

 INTRODUCTION

We discussed in the last chapter that technology will address what appear to be technological problems, but not human behavior. There are currently many capabilities available from various cybersecurity solutions to mitigate technical cyber threats. Traditional cybersecurity measures no longer ensure adequate information, data, and network security. As the last four chapters show, adverse cyber incidents negatively impact organizations' confidentiality, integrity, and availability. These incidents may be purposeful or inadvertent ones caused by misconfigured software, human errors, misaligned cyber-security strategy, or a combination of factors. This is where cyber resilience comes in. Cyber Resilience, What is it? Why should BOD members and C-LEs understand cyber resilience now? Organizations, in general, have a severe problem. They don't typically know which elements of their infrastructure are vulnerable, how deep the cyber-attackers are, what access they have, and what tools they are using. Cyber resilience helps to provide insight into whether an organization can respond technologically to a cyber disruption and restore business operations. Cyber-attackers are stealing more from us than ever before, so the ability to identify, protect, detect, respond to, and recover from a cyber-attack is just as important as trying to block it.

Data breaches have been growing over the last few years. In fact, according to IBM, "the most common initial attack vector, compromised credentials, was responsible for 20% of breaches at an average breach cost of USD 4.37 million."[1]

Beyond this financial impact, every BOD member and C-level executive has an obligation and responsibility to limit the impact of cyber-crime on the company's brand, finance, legal, and customer trust obligations. In most cases, cyber resilience receives limited attention, resources, or executive focus until an actual significant threat appears. Every organization needs to build resilience into every part of its business, from business process mapping to engineering service availability and critical vendor dependency.

Organizations across the globe are undergoing a digital transformation related to hyper-convergence, which is creating unintended gateways for cyber risks, vulnerabilities, attacks, and failures. The BOD members and C-level executives must acknowledge that a cyber-resilient strategy is necessary. This strategy must recognize that different data types and categories do not intrinsically hold the same value. They also should not have the same level of investment when it comes to cybersecurity strategy. A cyber-resiliency strategy helps businesses apply the appropriate resources to reduce cyber risks, financial impact, and reputational damage. A technology-centric approach unifies cyber risk management precepts from all the chapters in this book. Cyber resilience as part of the cyber strategy helps businesses protect business-critical infrastructure. Being aware of cyber risks, in turn, minimizes nonconformity to legislation or privacy laws and speeds up recovery from a data breach or a similar disruption.

Cyber Resilience?

Being resilient to cyber-attacks and technology failures should be a foundational goal of any cybersecurity strategy and a critical precept that integrates all the approaches/precepts from the previous four chapters. Resilience is defined as follows:

- ▪ "Ensuring resilience—the ability to adapt to changing conditions and prepare for, withstand and rapidly recover from disruption—is a DHS (Department of Homeland Security) mission that all components and homeland security partners must work together to achieve." According to the DHS, "Whether it is resilience toward acts of terrorism, cyber-attacks, pandemics, and catastrophic natural disasters, our national preparedness is the shared responsibility of all levels of government, the private and nonprofit sectors, and individual citizens."[2]
- ▪ "Resilience is the ability to become successful again after something bad happens." —*Merriam-Webster Dictionary*[3]

Without enough resilience, a cyber-attack or failure might cause considerable harm or even force an organization to go out of business. This undoubtedly makes cyber resilience one of any organization's most important cyber-security strategies. Suppose resilience is the ability of an organization to rapidly respond to business disruptions and restore business operations in a timely fashion. In such a situation, we define cyber resilience as the capacity to adapt by leveraging the organization's cyber capabilites to restore operational processes within changing conditions. Cyber resilience implies that an organization can withstand external shocks, but it also means that the critical infrastructure and applications it employs are also resilient. This places a greater emphasis on cybersecurity to protect an organization's crown jewels, thus providing overall protection. The capacity to foresee, tolerate, recover from, and adapt to adverse situations, pressures, assaults, or breaches of cyber resources is referred to as cyber resilience.

THE VALUE PROPOSITION OF CYBER RESILIENCE

You are going to be attacked; your computers are going to be attacked, and the question is, how do you fight through the attack? How do you maintain your operations?

—Lt. Gen. Ted F. Bowlds, former commander, Electronic Systems Center, USAF

The fundamental purpose of cyber resilience is to fulfil the demands of stakeholders while reducing cyber risks to organizational goals and objectives. The ability to predict, withstand, and adapt to cyber-attacks is referred to as cyber resilience. The BOD and C-LEs should assume that threat actors have already compromised the organization and that their organization is under assault or will be victimized soon.

Below is a summary outline of the value proposition of cyber resilience and how it sums up the last four chapters of this book.

Cybersecurity Strategy: Cyber resiliency enhances cybersecurity strategy. Cyber resilience is helpful for more than just responding to and surviving an assault. It may also assist an organization in formulating strategies to improve IT governance, nurture cybersecurity across critical assets, strengthen data protection initiatives, mitigate the effects of natural catastrophes, and eliminate some human error. One of the underappreciated advantages of cyber resilience is that it enhances the day-to-day operations of cybersecurity teams. A hands-on cybersecurity staff increases an organization's capacity to respond to attacks and helps to guarantee that day-to-day operations function smoothly.

Cyber Value: Cyber resilience significantly reduces financial loss. No matter how excellent an organization's cybersecurity is, the truth remains that no one is immune to cyber-attacks. The average cost of a cyber event has surged into the millions of dollars globally, enough to bankrupt many small- to medium-sized organizations. Besides financial expenses, the reputational effect of data breaches is growing because of the implementation of privacy laws and other data protection and privacy regulatory requirements in various countries and strict data breach reporting requirements. Inadequate cyber resilience can permanently harm an organization's reputation. Cyber resilience protects a corporation against public scrutiny, regulatory fines, a sudden drop in revenues, or worse, loss of business. It increases trust within the business environment. It is critical to have cyber resilience to sustain supplier and customer confidence. It takes years to create trust, yet it can be lost instantly. If a company's cyber resilience plan is inadequate, it may suffer substantial deleterious effects, such as reimbursing suppliers and customers whose confidentiality was compromised.

Cyber Compliance: Cyber resilience helps organizations achieve regulatory and legal compliance. Meeting data protection and critical infrastructure regulatory security criteria is a competitive advantage and a valuable benefit of incorporating cyber resilience into a company. The EU Network and Information Systems (NIS) security directive, for example, requires every operator of critical infrastructure (such as finance, healthcare, transportation, water and electric grid, and aviation) to "take appropriate security measures and to notify serious incidents to the relevant national authority." The GDPR demands strong safeguards to protect data privacy and charges massive fines for violations. Customers are more likely to trust businesses if organizations comply with legislation.

Cyber Culture: Cyber resilience fosters a more cyber-secure culture. Everyone is responsible for cybersecurity. Critical information and critical assets are less in danger when individuals are inspired and motivated to take security seriously in their firm. To prevent human mistakes that expose sensitive data, the business should promote correct security behavior.

The BOD members and C-LEs must articulate how the organization can withstand a cyber-attack while maintaining core business operations. Finally, they must also ensure that the cyber resilience risk management plan will constantly be adjusted by mapping any changes to the business's goals and objectives to the evolving threat landscape.

 ## CASE STUDIES

The rise in the frequency of cyber-attacks, along with the relative cost of a breach, has heightened the threats for businesses, particularly those posed by complex, focused cyber-attacks on the industry's high-profile, high-value information, critical infrastructure, and intellectual property. This section reflects on a few high-profile examples to illustrate why cyber resilience is a foundational precept.

The Sony Pictures Data Breach

In November 2014, a hacker group leaked a large amount of confidential data from Sony Pictures. The data included personal information about employees and their families, emails between employees, information about executives' salaries, copies of yet-unreleased Sony films, and other sensitive information.

According to the *Washington Post*, "While the news has been dominated by big retail hacks over the past year, the Sony Pictures cyber-attack was much more disruptive: It knocked out computer systems at the company, and the fallout from the wholesale distribution of internal documents is far different from having to respond to the theft of credit card numbers. Many within the cybersecurity community hope this will act as a wake-up call to the companies about their vulnerability to digital adversaries—both in terms of beefing up their current defenses and their back-up capabilities."[4]

Shortly after the data breach, the CEO resigned, which can be another major consequence of large cyber failures.

The Equifax Data Breach

In March 2017, over 147 million credit records were stolen from the American credit bureau, Equifax. According to the *Washington Post*, hackers exploited a "website application vulnerability" and obtained personal data about British and Canadian consumers as well as Americans.[5] "Social Security numbers and birth dates are particularly sensitive data, giving those who possess them the ingredients for identity fraud and other crimes. Equifax also lost control of an unspecified number of driver's licenses, along with the credit card numbers for 209,000 consumers and credit dispute documents for 182,000 others."

This resulted in Equifax having to incur over a billion dollars in recovery costs and settlements with US regulators in 2019. It is no surprise that Equifax will still need to invest millions of dollars more in cyber risk management in the foreseeable future.

The Capital One Data Breach

In 2019, in one of the biggest data breaches ever, a hacker gained access to more than 100 million Capital One customer accounts and credit card applications. Capital One, a large US bank, had misconfigured its web application firewall, allowing a hacker to exploit it and generate a fraudulent access token. The hacker was then able to exfiltrate millions of personal data records. According to the *Washington Post*, "The Capital One hack was one of the largest data breaches ever to hit a financial services firm. The credit-reporting company Equifax disclosed that hackers had stolen the personal information of 147 million people."[6] It cost Capital One millions of dollars to settle the federal bank regulators' claims.

The Colonial Pipeline Data Breach

The Colonial Pipeline data breach is discussed in Chapter 2, and it's discussed here as well, this time from a technology-centric point of view. As you may recall, in May 2021, one of the largest petroleum pipelines in the United States was reportedly breached. Colonial Pipeline shut down its massive oil pipeline after a ransomware attack took some of its systems offline. It appears to be the largest ever cyber-attack on an American energy system and yet another example of cybersecurity vulnerabilities that President Joe Biden has promised to address.

According to *Bloomberg,* "On May 7, an employee in Colonial's control room saw a ransom note demanding cryptocurrency appear on a computer just before 5 a.m. The employee notified an operations supervisor who immediately began to start the process of shutting down the pipeline, Colonial Chief Executive Officer Joseph Blount said in an interview. By 6:10 a.m., the entire pipeline had been shut down, Blount said, 'It was the first time Colonial had shut down the entirety of its gasoline pipeline system in its 57-year history. We had no choice at that point. It was absolutely the right thing to do. At that time, we had no idea who was attacking us or what their motives were.'"[7]

Ransomware attacks generally use malware to lock companies out of their systems until a ransom is paid. Such attacks have surged in the past few years and cost organizations billions of dollars just in ransoms paid, not counting those that aren't reported or any costs associated with having systems offline until the ransom is paid. Ransomware attacks have targeted groups in all areas, from the private to the public sector. The latter are especially attractive targets, given how urgent it is to get their systems back up as soon as possible.

The examples outlined in this section are extraordinary because none of those organizations was ready for a cyber-attack. The scale of each cyber breach should be a wake-up call for the BOD members and C-LEs to be cognizant of the magnitude and potential impact of this issue. Regrettably, there is no single adversary or threat to every business or industry's critical information and infrastructure, and there is no silver bullet for cybersecurity. Attackers range from basic script kiddies to threat actors and cybercriminals, as well as terrorists and state-sponsored hackers, each with their own set of abilities, toolkits, and motivations.

THREAT ACTORS?

The case studies highlight the compromised areas that threat actors leveraged from different vulnerabilities. This brings us to question: "What and who are the threat actors?" A threat actor is a person or entity responsible for a cybersecurity event. We refer them to as "actors" since it is a neutral phrase that avoids identifying them as a person, a group, or a collection of many groups. The term does not attribute motives to the actor, such as criminal activity or espionage. The word "threat actor" differs from "hacker" or "attacker" in that, unlike a hacker, a threat actor does not always have hacking or technical abilities. They are essentially malevolent entities attempting to compromise an organization's security. This might range from transferring private data onto a USB stick to physically destroying an organization's servers. It is a broad phrase that encompasses both internal and external risks. Having stated that, several threats exist. Many threat actors are technically skilled.

Although various motivations—notoriety, money, corporate advantage, or military superiority—can influence the actors' choice of targets, the linked structure of our globe implies that any organization may become a target of these adversaries. The biggest Internet attackers are no longer technologically gifted but are often opportunistic adolescents or online political demonstrators. They are still with us, but criminal attacks are more organized and well-funded than ever.

As threat actors have discovered how effective new cyber-resilience technologies are, they are altering their attack vectors and attacking people and processes. Threat actors are more skilled attackers whose purpose is to steal secrets or wage clandestine cyber warfare. They have the knowledge and resources to overcome even the most sophisticated technical defenses. Some of these robust cyber-attack vectors are currently in private hands.

What does this have to do with you? It means that for the foreseeable future, massive cybersecurity breaches are unavoidable for every firm linked to the Internet. Executives must be ready to handle cyber challenges efficiently and continue business operations, precisely as they do when a creative new competitor appears or when an organization loses a significant client or financing source.

Cyber resilience is the capacity to endure and rapidly recover from cyberattacks and other cyber-related incidents. The BOD and C-LEs need to clearly outline cyber resilience as an objective within the organization's cyber strategy.

Hackers with low skill, motivation, and resources pose a lower risk than well-financed, highly motivated, more sophisticated criminals and statesponsored groups. The risk an organization faces is also determined by the maturity of its cyber resilience, articulation of critical information and infrastructure, cyber risk culture, cyber compliance, the impact of a breach, and the vulnerabilities present.

The organization should design defenses in this manner. The well-known firewalls and classic signature-based antivirus do not fully defend crown jewels, critical information, and infrastructure. They remain essential technologies for removing a large swath of opportunistic low-level assaults. Their use allows the cyber-resilience technology strategy, intelligent security technologies, and humans to cope with the more severe risks of attack vectors from skilled attackers. This implies that the BOD and C-LEs must ensure a suitable level of investment to prepare an organization to defend itself against a broad spectrum of threat actors. It is a complex undertaking, but the notion of risk-based security makes it more workable.

EXECUTIVE'S GUIDE TO CYBER RESILIENCE

It is now clear that the networks of most organizations have been compromised across different industries and organizations. The responsibility of BOD members and C-LEs to support and envisage the need of cyber resilience will remain for the foreseeable future. It is more expensive and complicated to be reactive than to have foresight about cyber risk management. It could be years before organizations are cyber-secure again if BOD members and C-LEs do not make cyber resilience a strategic priority. Malicious actors will still destroy or alter data and impersonate legitimate people in organizations. Not only are the examples in this chapter among the most high-profile examples of cyber breaches in recent memory, but they also should serve as wake-up calls to any BOD member and C-LE.

Without focused prioritization, sufficient funding, and cybersecurity teams tasked to lead an organization-wide cyber resilience strategy, an attack can blindside an organization. Cyber-attacks should speed up a broad change in mindset, making cyber resilience a top priority by turning to a new way of thinking (foresight). Executives must assume that there are already breaches rather than merely reacting to attacks after finding them (hindsight).

How Do Cybersecurity and Cyber Resilience Differ?

The distinction between cybersecurity and cyber resilience is critical. Cybersecurity is concerned with securing an organization from cyber-attacks. Firewalls, VPNs, anti-malware software, and hygiene, such as updating software and firmware and teaching personnel about secure behaviors, are all part of cybersecurity.

Cyber resilience works with cybersecurity. Most cyber resilience measures assume, leverage, or enhance various cybersecurity measures. Cybersecurity and cyber resilience measures are most effective when applied together in a balanced way. The cyber resilience perspective assumes that modern systems are large and complex entities, and the systems, operational environments, and supply chains will always have flaws and weaknesses that adversaries can exploit.

Given resource limitations, achieving sufficiently effective defense of systems and missions requires making trade-offs among measures to achieve cybersecurity objectives and cyber resilience objectives. Cyber resilience focuses on times when cybersecurity measures fail and when networks are interrupted by human error, power outages, or even just weather. Resilience considers where an organization's operations rely on technology, where critical data is stored, and how a disruption can affect those areas.

Resilience Includes Responding to Changing Conditions

Cyber-attackers have created changes in risk calculations by investing in larger, broader, and more complex malicious cyber activities. Cyber resilience means that an organization can dynamically adjust to and effectively withstand or recover from unprecedented conditions after any cyber incident. If the company is cyber resilient, it can ensure that the organization will withstand the problem and recover quickly if the business is interrupted by cyber-attacks/breaches, hacking, or internal actions that cause a technology failure.

Organizations must prepare for cyber defense and resilience against a wide range of potential cyber threats, including login theft, phishing, malware, and so on. Resilience combines information security, enterprise business continuity, and organization. Cyber resilience is about managing risk, not trying to eliminate it. Risks will never be eliminated, but focusing on appropriately prioritized cybersecurity threats is more effective.

Since cyber risks are often unpredictable or not preventable, having a cyber-preparedness action plan enables an organization to quickly identify and respond to incidents and cope with their impact. The ability of an organization to consistently achieve expected results in the face of adverse cyber incidents is cyber resilience.

A technology-centric approach focused on resilience to cyber risk is a strategic foresight augmented by a human-centric approach through training and education. All BOD members and C-LEs must spearhead both aspects.

The NIST defines cyber resilience as:

> The ability to anticipate, withstand, recover from, and adapt to adverse conditions, stresses, attacks, or compromises on systems that use or are enabled by cyber resources.
>
> —*NIST*[8]

Note that all the definitions of resilience discussed so far in this chapter have commonalities. Each expresses:

▪ A recurring pattern in dealing with situations or events that involve disruption, difficulties, mistakes, flaws, or failures.

When confronted with cyber events or conditions that cause disruption, adversity, and defects, the organization must consistently undertake the following goals of resiliency: recover, withstand (i.e., sustain or resist), adapt (i.e., evolve), and expect (i.e., prepare)

NEXT STEPS/REFLECTION

Executives are responsible for the organization and establishment of a crisis management capability; boards are responsible for safeguarding the governance and viability of the organization. So crisis management should be a central preoccupation for the board of every organization, small or large, local or global. Why, then, do we see so few boards actively participating in, overseeing and assuring crisis management in the way they do other risks and contingency plans?

—Deloitte, "The Board's Role in Crisis Management"[9]

As if we hadn't learned enough from the previous examples of cyber incidents, the sophistication of cyber-attacks has gone through the roof in the last few years. Attackers are using innovative technologies to enter corporate networks and access business-critical assets. In this environment, organizations must begin leveraging technology, such as next-generation web application firewalls (WAFs), to avoid the most complex and sophisticated assaults. Automation of security processes enables organizations to gain speed and scalability in the broader IT environment, thus increasing cyber risks.

How to Get Started

A framework is often the starting point for an organization's path toward cyber resilience. A few model frameworks, in particular the "Cyber Resiliency

Review" developed by the US Department of Homeland Security, NIST, and Gartner, have been issued to help organizations enhance cyber resiliency.

The "NIST Cybersecurity Framework," found on the NIST website,[10] has five high-level functions:

- *Identify* means developing the organizational understanding to manage cybersecurity risk.
- *Prevent* means developing and implementing the controls to stop cyber-attacks.
- *Detect* means knowing when a cybersecurity event happens.
- *Respond* means to act when a cybersecurity event is detected.
- *Recover* means to restore all capabilities and services that were impaired because of the cybersecurity event.

You can use this framework, or one like it, to start to develop your company's cyber resilience strategy.

Building Resilience into Your Organization

Cyber resilience necessitates abandoning the belief in impenetrable networks. Cyber resilience always assumes that attackers will disrupt business operations. Thus, strategies to prioritize, avoid, respond to, and recover from such attacks must be in place. To be effective, cyber risk management must be the responsibility of every employee, and security must integrate best practices into all elements of the organization.

Executives must understand that substantial cyber resilience is critical for an organization if that organization cannot withstand a significant cyber-attack. If a clearly articulated cyber resilience strategy is absent and an organization is faced with the growth in cyber risks that comes with greater reliance on digitization, that organization cannot be sure that it will be able to continue operations. To minimize the attack and perform a complete and timely investigation, the BOD must put a cyber-resilience strategy in place that addresses both the business and security sides of a disruption. Cyber resilience begins with mastering the fundamentals of cyber risk management.

The concepts of all four of the previous chapters are intertwined with cyber resilience. This includes cyber strategy and cyber culture, teaching personnel how to stay cyber-secure. If cyber resilience is already well adapted, it can ensure operational and business continuity while minimizing disruption. The truth is more difficult to nail down, since you must have confidence in your organization's capacity to respond to an assault, preserve customers' trust, absorb the financial, legal, and brand effects, and return to business. However, if there is no acknowledged cyber-resilience framework, there is no maturity model.

Most maturity models enable organizations to assess their capabilities and then transform digital assets, supply chains, cybersecurity, and data management. What would maturity in cyber resilience look like? It is not only about the capacity to respond and recover; it is also about how soon an organization can recover and what priorities it has. A mature cyber resilience strategy should be adaptive, agile, and constantly developing, creating a framework that specifies a collection of qualities that assist the company and its leadership in understanding what cyber resilience is and how it will be attained. This framework would explain a strategy and mindset for providing cyber resilience. Is the organization, for example, engaging in random acts of resilience? Creating a plan to look at it when an auditor requests it? True resilience entails a multifaceted approach that dynamically adapts to cyber risks while maintaining organization goals.

Start-ups, Small- and Medium-sized Businesses (SMBs)

Most, if not all, start-ups and small- and medium-sized businesses (SMBs) must keep expenses low while allowing their personnel to focus on their day jobs. However, because start-ups and SMBs are so focused on growth, they may overlook the importance of data security, not recognizing that a breach or outage can have significant long-term consequences. The more users there are in an organization, the greater the threat landscape for criminals to enter.

The four main preliminary actions that every start-up or SMB may take to construct cyber resilience are:

1. Establishing a Framework: The method of creating cyber resilience varies from organization to organization. Establishing a framework is an effective method to start an organization's journey to become cyber-resilient. A framework will guide how to develop priorities and objectives for cyber resilience initiatives and establish a focused, scalable, and cost-effective route to being cyber-resilient.
2. Risk Assessment: The second stage in developing a robust cyber resilience approach is identifying cyber risks. Cyber resilience aims to ensure the long-term viability of business operations. Make a list of where activities rely on technology to understand better how a cyber-attack will affect the business.

3. Resource Evaluation: Analyze business resources after a risk assessment to see whether an organization might benefit from a managed service provider or additional automation. Make a count of both human and technological capital within the business.

4. Identification, Protection, and Detection: The final stage is to develop a cyber-attack defense strategy based on the business's most critical business operations assets (and how a successful cyber-attack could impact them). Take measures to identify and protect against cyber risks, but keep in mind that early identification can reduce the impact of a cyber-attack on business activities.

A robust cyber resilience strategy empowers executives to foresee a compromise and decide what is and is not a priority. A governance structure, complete with policies and processes, may be integrated into business strategy. This organization-specific cyber resilience framework is evaluated regularly to ensure that it remains relevant in the face of emerging challenges. There are many frameworks available to construct and assess cyber resilience. Still, in this case, the recommendation is NIST SP 800-160 Vol. by the U.S. Department of Homeland Security 2, which may be found for further reference in Appendix E.

SUMMARY

I want to end this book with a couple of thoughts. Every board and senior management agenda should include a discussion of the five precepts outlined in the book. Given all you've read in this book, is it not time for the BODs, C-Level executives, and governments to step up and notice the external environment of cyber threats and secure the future starting today?

This means continually strengthening resistance to ever-increasing cyber risks and ensuring cyber risk management now and in the future for a cyber-secure digital society and global economy. A call for action for all BODs and C-LEs is to prioritize and include cyber risk management as an agenda item at a high standard level to increase cyber resilience and incident response capacities.

Cyber-attacks in the public and private sectors will continue to skyrocket because we live in an increasingly digitalized environment. The stakes are enormous, and fresh insights and shifts in mindset are vital to bolstering cyber risk management. Building cybersecurity resilience into a business means balancing investments across the cyber risk management lifecycle, diligently applying maintenance, reacting to anomalies and alarms to minimize harmful effects, and maturing the cyber-resilience approach. Balancing cyber risk management investments will aid in the prevention of cyber-attacks and the speedy restoration of business operations despite a successful cyber-attack. By investing in cyber resilience, you can lead the way to reduce your organization's cyber risk.

NOTES

1. https://www.ibm.com/security/data-breach
2. https://www.dhs.gov/xlibrary/hsin-annual-report-2017/partnerships/introduction.html
3. https://www.merriam-webster.com/dictionary/resilience#:~:text=1%20%3A%20the%20ability%20to%20become,%2C%20pressed%2C%20bent%2C%20etc.
4. https://www.washingtonpost.com/news/the-switch/wp/2014/12/18/the-sony-pictures-hack-explained/
5. https://www.washingtonpost.com/business/technology/equifax-hack-hits-credit-histories-of-up-to-143-million-americans/2017/09/07/a4ae6f82-941a-11e7-b9bc-b2f7903bab0d_story.html
6. https://www.washingtonpost.com/national-security/capital-one-fined-2019-hack/2020/08/06/90c2c836-d7f3-11ea-aff6-220dd3a14741_story.html
7. https://www.bloomberg.com/news/articles/2021-06-04/hackers-breached-colonial-pipeline-using-compromised-password
8. https://csrc.nist.gov/glossary/term/cyber_resiliency#:~:text=Definition(s)%3A,are%20enabled%20by%20cyber%20resources
9. https://www2.deloitte.com/content/dam/Deloitte/uk/Documents/risk/deloitte-uk-risk-global-on-the-boards-agenda-crisis-management.pdf
10. https://www.nist.gov/cyberframework

Appendix A: Framework for Improving Critical Infrastructure Cybersecurity

THIS FRAMEWORK IS THE result of an ongoing collaborative effort involving industry, academia, and government. The National Institute of Standards and Technology (NIST) launched the project by convening private- and public-sector organizations and individuals in 2013. Published in 2014 and revised during 2017 and 2018, this *Framework for Improving Critical Infrastructure Cybersecurity* has relied upon eight public workshops, multiple Requests for Comment or Information, and thousands of direct interactions with stakeholders from across all sectors of the United States along with many sectors from around the world.

To see the complete framework go to: https://doi.org/10.6028/NIST .CSWP.04162018. Framework for Improving Critical Infrastructure Cybersecurity 2018 / NIST / Public domain

 ## EXECUTIVE SUMMARY

The United States depends on the reliable functioning of critical infrastructure. Cybersecurity threats exploit the increased complexity and connectivity of critical infrastructure systems, placing the Nation's security, economy, and public safety and health at risk. Similar to financial and reputational risks, cybersecurity risk affects a company's bottom line. It can drive up costs and affect revenue. It can harm an organization's ability to innovate and to gain and maintain customers. Cybersecurity can be an important and amplifying component of an organization's overall risk management.

To better address these risks, the Cybersecurity Enhancement Act of 2014[1] (CEA) updated the role of the National Institute of Standards and Technology

(NIST) to include identifying and developing cybersecurity risk frameworks for voluntary use by critical infrastructure owners and operators. Through CEA, NIST must identify "a prioritized, flexible, repeatable, performance- based, and cost-effective approach, including information security measures and controls that may be voluntarily adopted by owners and operators of critical infrastructure to help them identify, assess, and manage cyber risks." This formalized NIST's previous work developing Framework Version 1.0 under Executive Order (EO) 13636, "Improving Critical Infrastructure Cybersecurity" (February 2013), and provided guidance for future Framework evolution. The Framework that was developed under EO 13636, and continues to evolve according to CEA, uses a common language to address and manage cybersecurity risk in a cost-effective way based on business and organizational needs without placing additional regulatory requirements on businesses.

The Framework focuses on using business drivers to guide cybersecurity activities and considering cybersecurity risks as part of the organization's risk management processes. The Framework consists of three parts: the Framework Core, the Implementation Tiers, and the Framework Profiles. The Framework Core is a set of cybersecurity activities, outcomes, and informative references that are common across sectors and critical infrastructure. Elements of the Core provide detailed guidance for developing individual organizational Profiles. Through use of Profiles, the Framework will help an organization to align and prioritize its cybersecurity activities with its business/mission requirements, risk tolerances, and resources. The Tiers provide a mechanism for organizations to view and understand the characteristics of their approach to managing cybersecurity risk, which will help in prioritizing and achieving cybersecurity objectives.

While this document was developed to improve cybersecurity risk management in critical infrastructure, the Framework can be used by organizations in any sector or community. The Framework enables organizations – regardless of size, degree of cybersecurity risk, or cybersecurity sophistication – to apply the principles and best practices of risk management to improving security and resilience.

The Framework provides a common organizing structure for multiple approaches to cybersecurity by assembling standards, guidelines, and practices that are working effectively today. Moreover, because it references globally recognized standards for cybersecurity, the

Framework can serve as a model for international cooperation on strengthening cybersecurity in critical infrastructure as well as other sectors and communities.

The Framework offers a flexible way to address cybersecurity, including cybersecurity's effect on physical, cyber, and people dimensions. It is applicable to organizations relying on technology, whether their cybersecurity focus is primarily on information technology (IT), industrial control systems (ICS), cyber-physical systems (CPS), or connected devices more generally, including the Internet of Things (IoT). The Framework can assist organizations in addressing cybersecurity as it affects the privacy of customers, employees, and other parties.

Additionally, the Framework's outcomes serve as targets for workforce development and evolution activities.

The Framework is not a one-size-fits-all approach to managing cybersecurity risk for critical infrastructure. Organizations will continue to have unique risks – different threats, different vulnerabilities, different risk tolerances. They also will vary in how they customize practices described in the Framework. Organizations can determine activities that are important to critical service delivery and can prioritize investments to maximize the impact of each dollar spent.

Ultimately, the Framework is aimed at reducing and better managing cybersecurity risks.

To account for the unique cybersecurity needs of organizations, there are a wide variety of ways to use the Framework. The decision about how to apply it is left to the implementing organization. For example, one organization may choose to use the Framework Implementation Tiers to articulate envisioned risk management practices. Another organization may use the Framework's five Functions to analyze its entire risk management portfolio; that analysis may or may not rely on more detailed companion guidance, such as controls catalogs. There sometimes is discussion about "compliance" with the Framework, and the Framework has utility as a structure and language for organizing and expressing compliance with an organization's own cybersecurity requirements. Nevertheless, the variety of ways in which the Framework can be used by an organization means that phrases like "compliance with the Framework" can be confusing and mean something very different to various stakeholders.

The Framework is a living document and will continue to be updated and improved as industry provides feedback on implementation. NIST will continue coordinating with the private sector and government agencies at all levels. As the Framework is put into greater practice, additional lessons learned will be integrated into future versions. This will ensure the Framework is meeting the needs of critical infrastructure owners and operators in a dynamic and challenging environment of new threats, risks, and solutions.

Expanded and more effective use and sharing of best practices of this voluntary Framework are the next steps to improve the cybersecurity of our Nation's critical infrastructure – providing evolving guidance for individual organizations while increasing the cybersecurity posture of the Nation's critical infrastructure and the broader economy and society.

1.0 FRAMEWORK INTRODUCTION

The United States depends on the reliable functioning of its critical infrastructure. Cybersecurity threats exploit the increased complexity and connectivity of critical infrastructure systems, placing the Nation's security, economy, and public safety and health at risk. Similar to financial and reputational risks, cybersecurity risk affects a company's bottom line. It can drive up costs and affect revenue. It can harm an organization's ability to innovate and to gain and maintain customers. Cybersecurity can be an important and amplifying component of an organization's overall risk management.

To strengthen the resilience of this infrastructure, the Cybersecurity Enhancement Act of 2014[2] (CEA) updated the role of the National Institute of Standards and Technology (NIST) to "facilitate and support the development of" cybersecurity risk frameworks. Through CEA, NIST must identify "a prioritized, flexible, repeatable, performance-based, and cost-effective approach, including information security measures and controls that may be voluntarily adopted by owners and operators of critical infrastructure to help them identify, assess, and manage cyber risks." This formalized NIST's previous work developing Framework Version 1.0 under Executive Order 13636, "Improving Critical Infrastructure Cybersecurity," issued in February 2013[3], and provided guidance for future Framework evolution.

Critical infrastructure[4] is defined in the U.S. Patriot Act of 2001[5] as "systems and assets, whether physical or virtual, so vital to the United States that the incapacity or destruction of such systems and assets would have a debilitating impact on security, national economic security, national public health or safety, or any combination of those matters." Due to the increasing pressures from external and internal threats, organizations responsible for critical infrastructure need to have a consistent and iterative approach to identifying, assessing, and managing cybersecurity risk. This approach is necessary regardless of an organization's size, threat exposure, or cybersecurity sophistication today.

The critical infrastructure community includes public and private owners and operators, and other entities with a role in securing the Nation's infrastructure. Members of each critical infrastructure sector perform functions that are supported by the broad category of technology, including information technology (IT), industrial control systems (ICS), cyber-physical systems (CPS), and connected devices more generally, including the Internet of Things (IoT). This reliance on technology, communication, and interconnectivity has changed and expanded the potential vulnerabilities and increased potential risk to operations. For example, as technology and the data it produces and processes are increasingly used to deliver critical services and support business/mission decisions, the potential impacts of a cybersecurity incident on an organization, the health and safety of individuals, the environment, communities, and the broader economy and society should be considered.

To manage cybersecurity risks, a clear understanding of the organization's business drivers and security considerations specific to its use of technology is required. Because each organization's risks, priorities, and systems are unique, the tools and methods used to achieve the outcomes described by the Framework will vary.

Recognizing the role that the protection of privacy and civil liberties plays in creating greater public trust, the Framework includes a methodology to protect individual privacy and civil liberties when critical infrastructure organizations conduct cybersecurity activities. Many organizations already have processes for addressing privacy and civil liberties. The methodology is designed to complement such processes and provide guidance to facilitate privacy risk management consistent with an organization's approach to cybersecurity risk management.

Integrating privacy and cybersecurity can benefit organizations by increasing customer confidence, enabling more standardized sharing of information, and simplifying operations across legal regimes.

The Framework remains effective and supports technical innovation because it is technology neutral, while also referencing a variety of existing standards, guidelines, and practices that evolve with technology. By relying on those global standards, guidelines, and practices developed, managed, and updated by industry, the tools and methods available to achieve the Framework outcomes will scale across borders, acknowledge the global nature of cybersecurity risks, and evolve with technological advances and business requirements. The use of existing and emerging standards will enable economies of scale and drive the development of effective products, services, and practices that meet identified market needs. Market competition also promotes faster diffusion of these technologies and practices and realization of many benefits by the stakeholders in these sectors.

Building from those standards, guidelines, and practices, the Framework provides a common taxonomy and mechanism for organizations to:

1. Describe their current cybersecurity posture;
2. Describe their target state for cybersecurity;
3. Identify and prioritize opportunities for improvement within the context of a continuous and repeatable process;
4. Assess progress toward the target state;
5. Communicate among internal and external stakeholders about cybersecurity risk.

The Framework is not a one-size-fits-all approach to managing cybersecurity risk for critical infrastructure. Organizations will continue to have unique risks – different threats, different vulnerabilities, different risk tolerances. They also will vary in how they customize practices described in the Framework. Organizations can determine activities that are important to critical service delivery and can prioritize investments to maximize the impact of each dollar spent.

Ultimately, the Framework is aimed at reducing and better managing cybersecurity risks.

To account for the unique cybersecurity needs of organizations, there are a wide variety of ways to use the Framework. The decision about how to apply it is left to the implementing organization. For example, one organization may choose to use the Framework Implementation Tiers to articulate envisioned risk management practices. Another organization may use the Framework's five Functions to analyze its entire risk management portfolio; that analysis may or may not rely on more detailed companion guidance, such as controls catalogs. There sometimes is discussion about "compliance" with the Framework, and the Framework has utility as a structure and language for organizing and expressing compliance with an organization's own cybersecurity requirements. Nevertheless, the variety of ways in which the Framework can be used by an organization means that phrases like "compliance with the Framework" can be confusing and mean something very different to various stakeholders.

The Framework complements, and does not replace, an organization's risk management process and cybersecurity program. The organization can use its current processes and leverage the Framework to identify opportunities to strengthen and communicate its management of cybersecurity risk while aligning with industry practices. Alternatively, an organization without an existing cybersecurity program can use the Framework as a reference to establish one.

While the Framework has been developed to improve cybersecurity risk management as it relates to critical infrastructure, it can be used by organizations in any sector of the economy or society. It is intended to be useful to companies, government agencies, and not-for-profit organizations regardless of their focus or size. The common taxonomy of standards, guidelines, and practices that it provides also is not country-specific. Organizations outside the United States may also use the Framework to strengthen their own cybersecurity efforts, and the Framework can contribute to developing a common language for international cooperation on critical infrastructure cybersecurity.

1.1 OVERVIEW OF THE FRAMEWORK

The Framework is a risk-based approach to managing cybersecurity risk, and is composed of three parts: the Framework Core, the Framework Implementation Tiers, and the Framework Profiles. Each Framework component reinforces the connection between business/mission drivers and cybersecurity activities. These components are explained below.

■ The *Framework Core* is a set of cybersecurity activities, desired outcomes, and applicable references that are common across critical infrastructure sectors. The Core presents industry standards, guidelines, and practices in a manner that allows for communication of cybersecurity activities and outcomes across the organization from the executive level to the implementation/operations level. The Framework Core consists of five concurrent and continuous Functions—Identify, Protect, Detect, Respond, Recover. When considered together, these Functions provide a high-level, strategic view of the lifecycle of an organization's management of cybersecurity risk. The Framework Core then identifies underlying key Categories and Subcategories – which are discrete outcomes – for each Function, and matches them with example Informative References such as existing standards, guidelines, and practices for each Subcategory.

■ *Framework Implementation Tiers* ("Tiers") provide context on how an organization views cybersecurity risk and the processes in place to manage that risk. Tiers describe the degree to which an organization's cybersecurity risk management practices exhibit the characteristics defined in the Framework (e.g., risk and threat aware, repeatable, and adaptive).

The Tiers characterize an organization's practices over a range, from Partial (Tier 1) to Adaptive (Tier 4). These Tiers reflect a progression from informal, reactive responses to approaches that are agile and risk-informed. During the Tier selection process, an organization should consider its current risk management practices, threat environment, legal and regulatory requirements, business/mission objectives, and organizational constraints.

▦ A *Framework Profile* ("Profile") represents the outcomes based on business needs that an organization has selected from the Framework Categories and Subcategories. The Profile can be characterized as the alignment of standards, guidelines, and practices to the Framework Core in a particular implementation scenario. Profiles can be used to identify opportunities for improving cybersecurity posture by comparing a "Current" Profile (the "as is" state) with a "Target" Profile (the "to be" state). To develop a Profile, an organization can review all of the Categories and Subcategories and, based on business/mission drivers and a risk assessment, determine which are most important; it can add Categories and Subcategories as needed to address the organization's risks. The Current Profile can then be used to support prioritization and measurement of progress toward the Target Profile, while factoring in other business needs including cost- effectiveness and innovation. Profiles can be used to conduct self-assessments and communicate within an organization or between organizations.

1.2 RISK MANAGEMENT AND THE CYBERSECURITY FRAMEWORK

Risk management is the ongoing process of identifying, assessing, and responding to risk. To manage risk, organizations should understand the likelihood that an event will occur and the potential resulting impacts. With this information, organizations can determine the acceptable level of risk for achieving their organizational objectives and can express this as their risk tolerance.

With an understanding of risk tolerance, organizations can prioritize cybersecurity activities, enabling organizations to make informed decisions about cybersecurity expenditures.

Implementation of risk management programs offers organizations the ability to quantify and communicate adjustments to their cybersecurity programs.

Organizations may choose to handle risk in different ways, including mitigating the risk, transferring the risk, avoiding the risk, or accepting the risk, depending on the potential impact to the delivery of critical services. The Framework uses risk management processes to enable organizations to inform and prioritize decisions regarding cybersecurity. It supports recurring risk assessments and validation of business drivers to help organizations select target states for cybersecurity activities that reflect desired outcomes. Thus, the Framework gives organizations the ability to dynamically select and direct improvement in cybersecurity risk management for the IT and ICS environments.

The Framework is adaptive to provide a flexible and risk-based implementation that can be used with a broad array of cybersecurity risk management processes. Examples of cybersecurity risk management processes include International Organization for Standardization (ISO) 31000:2009[6], ISO/International Electrotechnical Commission (IEC) 27005:2011[7], NIST Special Publication (SP) 800-39[8], and the *Electricity Subsector Cybersecurity Risk Management Process* (RMP) guideline[9].

 ## 2.0 FRAMEWORK BASICS

The Framework provides a common language for understanding, managing, and expressing cybersecurity risk to internal and external stakeholders. It can be used to help identify and prioritize actions for reducing cybersecurity risk, and it is a tool for aligning policy, business, and technological approaches to managing that risk. It can be used to manage cybersecurity risk across entire organizations or it can be focused on the delivery of critical services within an organization. Different types of entities – including sector coordinating structures, associations, and organizations – can use the Framework for different purposes, including the creation of common Profiles.

 ## 2.1 1 FRAMEWORK CORE

The *Framework Core* provides a set of activities to achieve specific cybersecurity *outcomes*, and references examples of guidance to achieve those outcomes. The Core is not a checklist of actions to perform. It presents key cybersecurity outcomes identified by stakeholders as helpful in managing cybersecurity risk. The

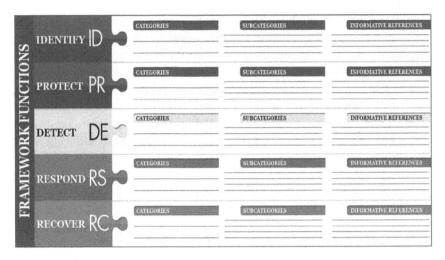

FIGURE 1   Framework Core Structure

Core comprises four elements: Functions, Categories, Subcategories, and Informative References, depicted in **Figure 1**:
The Framework Core elements work together as follows:

▩ **Functions** organize basic cybersecurity activities at their highest level. These Functions are Identify, Protect, Detect, Respond, and Recover. They aid an organization in expressing its management of cybersecurity risk by organizing information, enabling risk management decisions, addressing threats, and improving by learning from previous activities. The Functions also align with existing methodologies for incident management and help show the impact of investments in cybersecurity. For example, investments in planning and exercises support timely response and recovery actions, resulting in reduced impact to the delivery of services.

▩ **Categories** are the subdivisions of a Function into groups of cybersecurity outcomes closely tied to programmatic needs and particular activities. Examples of Categories include "Asset Management," "Identity Management and Access Control," and "Detection Processes."

▩ **Subcategories** further divide a Category into specific outcomes of technical and/or management activities. They provide a set of results that, while not exhaustive, help support achievement of the outcomes in each Category. Examples of Subcategories include "External information systems are catalogued," "Data-at-rest is protected," and "Notifications from detection systems are investigated."

■ **Informative References** are specific sections of standards, guidelines, and practices common among critical infrastructure sectors that illustrate a method to achieve the outcomes associated with each Subcategory. The Informative References presented in the Framework Core are illustrative and not exhaustive. They are based upon cross-sector guidance most frequently referenced during the Framework development process.

The five Framework Core Functions are defined below. These Functions are not intended to form a serial path or lead to a static desired end state. Rather, the Functions should be performed concurrently and continuously to form an operational culture that addresses the dynamic cybersecurity risk. See Appendix A for the complete Framework Core listing.

■ **Identify** – Develop an organizational understanding to manage cybersecurity risk to systems, people, assets, data, and capabilities.

The activities in the Identify Function are foundational for effective use of the Framework. Understanding the business context, the resources that support critical functions, and the related cybersecurity risks enables an organization to focus and prioritize its efforts, consistent with its risk management strategy and business needs. Examples of outcome Categories within this Function include: Asset Management; Business Environment; Governance; Risk Assessment; and Risk Management Strategy.

■ **Protect** – Develop and implement appropriate safeguards to ensure delivery of critical services.

The Protect Function supports the ability to limit or contain the impact of a potential cybersecurity event. Examples of outcome Categories within this Function include: Identity Management and Access Control; Awareness and Training; Data Security; Information Protection Processes and Procedures; Maintenance; and Protective Technology.

■ **Detect** – Develop and implement appropriate activities to identify the occurrence of a cybersecurity event.

The Detect Function enables timely discovery of cybersecurity events. Examples of outcome Categories within this Function include: Anomalies and Events; Security Continuous Monitoring; and Detection Processes.

▨ **Respond** – Develop and implement appropriate activities to take action regarding a detected cybersecurity incident.

The Respond Function supports the ability to contain the impact of a potential cybersecurity incident. Examples of outcome Categories within this Function include: Response Planning; Communications; Analysis; Mitigation; and Improvements.

▨ **Recover** – Develop and implement appropriate activities to maintain plans for resilience and to restore any capabilities or services that were impaired due to a cybersecurity incident.

The Recover Function supports timely recovery to normal operations to reduce the impact from a cybersecurity incident. Examples of outcome Categories within this Function include: Recovery Planning; Improvements; and Communications.

2.2 2 FRAMEWORK IMPLEMENTATION TIERS

The Framework Implementation Tiers ("Tiers") provide context on how an organization views cybersecurity risk and the processes in place to manage that risk. Ranging from Partial (Tier 1) to Adaptive (Tier 4), Tiers describe an increasing degree of rigor and sophistication in cybersecurity risk management practices. They help determine the extent to which cybersecurity risk management is informed by business needs and is integrated into an organization's overall risk management practices. Risk management considerations include many aspects of cybersecurity, including the degree to which privacy and civil liberties considerations are integrated into an organization's management of cybersecurity risk and potential risk responses.

The Tier selection process considers an organization's current risk management practices, threat environment, legal and regulatory requirements, information sharing practices, business/mission objectives, supply chain cybersecurity requirements, and organizational constraints.

Organizations should determine the desired Tier, ensuring that the selected level meets the organizational goals, is feasible to implement, and reduces cybersecurity risk to critical assets and resources to levels acceptable to the organization. Organizations should consider leveraging external guidance obtained from Federal government departments and agencies, Information Sharing and Analysis Centers (ISACs), Information Sharing and Analysis

Organizations (ISAOs), existing maturity models, or other sources to assist in determining their desired tier.

While organizations identified as Tier 1 (Partial) are encouraged to consider moving toward Tier 2 or greater, Tiers do not represent maturity levels. Tiers are meant to support organizational decision making about how to manage cybersecurity risk, as well as which dimensions of the organization are higher priority and could receive additional resources. Progression to higher Tiers is encouraged when a cost-benefit analysis indicates a feasible and cost-effective reduction of cybersecurity risk.

Successful implementation of the Framework is based upon achieving the outcomes described in the organization's Target Profile(s) and not upon Tier determination. Still, Tier selection and designation naturally affect Framework Profiles. The Tier recommendation by Business/Process Level managers, as approved by the Senior Executive Level, will help set the overall tone for how cybersecurity risk will be managed within the organization, and should influence prioritization within a Target Profile and assessments of progress in addressing gaps.

The Tier definitions are as follows:

Tier 1: Partial

- *Risk Management Process* – Organizational cybersecurity risk management practices are not formalized, and risk is managed in an *ad hoc* and sometimes reactive manner. Prioritization of cybersecurity activities may not be directly informed by organizational risk objectives, the threat environment, or business/mission requirements.
- *Integrated Risk Management Program* – There is limited awareness of cybersecurity risk at the organizational level. The organization implements cybersecurity risk management on an irregular, case-by-case basis due to varied experience or information gained from outside sources. The organization may not have processes that enable cybersecurity information to be shared within the organization.
- *External Participation* – The organization does not understand its role in the larger ecosystem with respect to either its dependencies or dependents. The organization does not collaborate with or receive information (e.g., threat intelligence, best practices, technologies) from other entities (e.g., buyers, suppliers, dependencies, dependents, ISAOs, researchers, governments), nor does it share information. The organization is generally unaware of the cyber supply chain risks of the products and services it provides and that it uses.

Tier 2: Risk Informed

▦ *Risk Management Process* – Risk management practices are approved by management but may not be established as organizational-wide policy. Prioritization of cybersecurity activities and protection needs is directly informed by organizational risk objectives, the threat environment, or business/mission requirements.

▦ *Integrated Risk Management Program* – There is an awareness of cybersecurity risk at the organizational level, but an organization-wide approach to managing cybersecurity risk has not been established. Cybersecurity information is shared within the organization on an informal basis. Consideration of cybersecurity in organizational objectives and programs may occur at some but not all levels of the organization. Cyber risk assessment of organizational and external assets occurs, but is not typically repeatable or reoccurring.

▦ *External Participation* – Generally, the organization understands its role in the larger ecosystem with respect to either its own dependencies or dependents, but not both. The organization collaborates with and receives some information from other entities and generates some of its own information, but may not share information with others. Additionally, the organization is aware of the cyber supply chain risks associated with the products and services it provides and uses, but does not act consistently or formally upon those risks.

Tier 3: Repeatable

▦ *Risk Management Process* – The organization's risk management practices are formally approved and expressed as policy. Organizational cybersecurity practices are regularly updated based on the application of risk management processes to changes in business/mission requirements and a changing threat and technology landscape.

▦ *Integrated Risk Management Program* – There is an organization-wide approach to manage cybersecurity risk. Risk-informed policies, processes, and procedures are defined, implemented as intended, and reviewed. Consistent methods are in place to respond effectively to changes in risk. Personnel possess the knowledge and skills to perform their appointed roles and responsibilities. The organization consistently and accurately monitors cybersecurity risk of organizational assets. Senior cybersecurity and non-cybersecurity executives communicate regularly regarding cybersecurity risk. Senior executives ensure consideration of cybersecurity through all lines of operation in the organization.

▩ *External Participation* – The organization understands its role, dependencies, and dependents in the larger ecosystem and may contribute to the community's broader understanding of risks. It collaborates with and receives information from other entities regularly that complements internally generated information, and shares information with other entities. The organization is aware of the cyber supply chain risks associated with the products and services it provides and that it uses. Additionally, it usually acts formally upon those risks, including mechanisms such as written agreements to communicate baseline requirements, governance structures (e.g., risk councils), and policy implementation and monitoring.

Tier 4: Adaptive

▩ *Risk Management Process* – The organization adapts its cybersecurity practices based on previous and current cybersecurity activities, including lessons learned and predictive indicators. Through a process of continuous improvement incorporating advanced cybersecurity technologies and practices, the organization actively adapts to a changing threat and technology landscape and responds in a timely and effective manner to evolving, sophisticated threats.

▩ *Integrated Risk Management Program* – There is an organization-wide approach to managing cybersecurity risk that uses risk-informed policies, processes, and procedures to address potential cybersecurity events. The relationship between cybersecurity risk and organizational objectives is clearly understood and considered when making decisions. Senior executives monitor cybersecurity risk in the same context as financial risk and other organizational risks. The organizational budget is based on an understanding of the current and predicted risk environment and risk tolerance. Business units implement executive vision and analyze system-level risks in the context of the organizational risk tolerances. Cybersecurity risk management is part of the organizational culture and evolves from an awareness of previous activities and continuous awareness of activities on their systems and networks. The organization can quickly and efficiently account for changes to business/mission objectives in how risk is approached and communicated.

▪ *External Participation* – The organization understands its role, dependencies, and dependents in the larger ecosystem and contributes to the community's broader understanding of risks. It receives, generates, and reviews prioritized information that informs continuous analysis of its risks as the threat and technology landscapes evolve. The organization shares that information internally and externally with other collaborators. The organization uses real-time or near real-time information to understand and consistently act upon cyber supply chain risks associated with the products and services it provides and that it uses. Additionally, it communicates proactively, using formal (e.g. agreements) and informal mechanisms to develop and maintain strong supply chain relationships.

2.3 3 FRAMEWORK PROFILE

The Framework Profile ("Profile") is the alignment of the Functions, Categories, and Subcategories with the business requirements, risk tolerance, and resources of the organization. A Profile enables organizations to establish a roadmap for reducing cybersecurity risk that is well aligned with organizational and sector goals, considers legal/regulatory requirements and industry best practices, and reflects risk management priorities. Given the complexity of many organizations, they may choose to have multiple profiles, aligned with particular components and recognizing their individual needs.

Framework Profiles can be used to describe the current state or the desired target state of specific cybersecurity activities. The Current Profile indicates the cybersecurity outcomes that are currently being achieved. The Target Profile indicates the outcomes needed to achieve the desired cybersecurity risk management goals. Profiles support business/mission requirements and aid in communicating risk within and between organizations. This Framework does not prescribe Profile templates, allowing for flexibility in implementation.

Comparison of Profiles (e.g., the Current Profile and Target Profile) may reveal gaps to be addressed to meet cybersecurity risk management objectives. An action plan to address these gaps to fulfill a given Category or Subcategory can contribute to the roadmap described above. Prioritizing the mitigation of gaps is driven by the organization's business needs and risk management processes. This risk-based approach enables an organization to gauge the resources needed (e.g., staffing, funding) to achieve cybersecurity goals in a cost-effective, prioritized manner. Furthermore, the Framework is a risk-based approach where the applicability and fulfillment of a given Subcategory is subject to the Profile's scope.

2.4 COORDINATION OF FRAMEWORK IMPLEMENTATION

Figure 2 describes a common flow of information and decisions at the following levels within an organization:

- ▪ Executive
- ▪ Business/Process
- ▪ Implementation/Operations

The executive level communicates the mission priorities, available resources, and overall risk tolerance to the business/process level. The business/process level uses the information as inputs into the risk management process, and then collaborates with the implementation/operations level to communicate business needs and create a Profile. The implementation/operations level communicates the Profile implementation progress to the business/process level. The business/process level uses this information to perform an impact

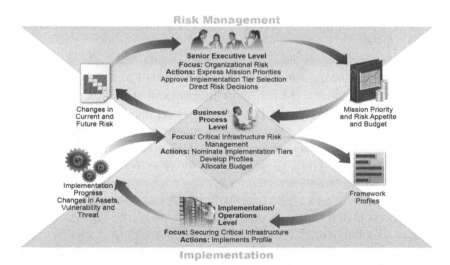

FIGURE 2   Notional Information and Decision Flows within an Organization
Source: National Institute of Standards and Technology

assessment. Business/process level management reports the outcomes of that impact assessment to the executive level to inform the organization's overall risk management process and to the implementation/operations level for awareness of business impact.

 ## 3.0 HOW TO USE THE FRAMEWORK

An organization can use the Framework as a key part of its systematic process for identifying, assessing, and managing cybersecurity risk. The Framework is not designed to replace existing processes; an organization can use its current process and overlay it onto the Framework to determine gaps in its current cybersecurity risk approach and develop a roadmap to improvement. Using the Framework as a cybersecurity risk management tool, an organization can determine activities that are most important to critical service delivery and prioritize expenditures to maximize the impact of the investment.

The Framework is designed to complement existing business and cybersecurity operations. It can serve as the foundation for a new cybersecurity program or a mechanism for improving an existing program. The Framework provides a means of expressing cybersecurity requirements to business partners and customers and can help identify gaps in an organization's cybersecurity practices. It also provides a general set of considerations and processes for considering privacy and civil liberties implications in the context of a cybersecurity program.

The Framework can be applied throughout the life cycle phases of plan, design, build/buy, deploy, operate, and decommission. The plan phase begins the cycle of any system and lays the groundwork for everything that follows. Overarching cybersecurity considerations should be declared and described as clearly as possible. The plan should recognize that those considerations and requirements are likely to evolve during the remainder of the life cycle. The design phase should account for cybersecurity requirements as a part of a larger multi- disciplinary systems engineering process.[10] A key milestone of the design phase is validation that the system cybersecurity specifications match the needs and risk disposition of the organization as captured in a Framework Profile. The desired cybersecurity outcomes prioritized in a Target Profile should be incorporated when a) developing the system during the build phase and b) purchasing or outsourcing the system during the buy phase. That same Target Profile serves as a list of system cybersecurity features that should be assessed when deploying the system to verify all features are implemented. The cybersecurity outcomes determined by using the Framework then should serve as a basis for ongoing operation of the system. This includes occasional reassessment, capturing results in a Current Profile, to verify that cybersecurity requirements are still fulfilled. Typically, a complex web of dependencies (e.g., compensating and common controls) among systems means the outcomes documented in Target Profiles of related systems should be carefully considered as systems are decommissioned.

The following sections present different ways in which organizations can use the Framework.

 ## 3.1 BASIC REVIEW OF CYBERSECURITY PRACTICES

The Framework can be used to compare an organization's current cybersecurity activities with those outlined in the Framework Core. Through the creation of a Current Profile, organizations can examine the extent to which they are achieving the outcomes described in the Core Categories and Subcategories, aligned with the five high-level Functions: Identify, Protect, Detect, Respond, and Recover. An organization may find that it is already achieving the desired outcomes, thus managing cybersecurity commensurate with the known risk. Alternatively, an organization may determine that it has opportunities to (or needs to) improve. The organization can use that information to develop an action plan to strengthen existing cybersecurity practices and reduce cybersecurity risk. An organization may also find that it is overinvesting to achieve certain outcomes. The organization can use this information to reprioritize resources.

While they do not replace a risk management process, these five high-level Functions will provide a concise way for senior executives and others to distill the fundamental concepts of cybersecurity risk so that they can assess how identified risks are managed, and how their organization stacks up at a high level against existing cybersecurity standards, guidelines, and practices. The Framework can also help an organization answer fundamental questions, including "How are we doing?" Then they can move in a more informed way to strengthen their cybersecurity practices where and when deemed necessary.

3.2 ESTABLISHING OR IMPROVING A CYBERSECURITY PROGRAM

The following steps illustrate how an organization could use the Framework to create a new cybersecurity program or improve an existing program. These steps should be repeated as necessary to continuously improve cybersecurity.

Step 1: Prioritize and Scope. The organization identifies its business/mission objectives and high-level organizational priorities. With this information, the organization makes strategic decisions regarding cybersecurity implementations and determines the scope of systems and assets that support the selected business line or process. The Framework can be adapted to support the different business lines or processes within an organization, which may have different business needs and associated risk tolerance. Risk tolerances may be reflected in a target Implementation Tier.

Step 2: Orient. Once the scope of the cybersecurity program has been determined for the business line or process, the organization identifies related systems and assets, regulatory requirements, and overall risk approach. The organization then consults sources to identify threats and vulnerabilities applicable to those systems and assets.

Step 3: Create a Current Profile. The organization develops a Current Profile by indicating which Category and Subcategory outcomes from the Framework Core are currently being achieved. If an outcome is partially achieved, noting this fact will help support subsequent steps by providing baseline information.

Step 4: Conduct a Risk Assessment. This assessment could be guided by the organization's overall risk management process or previous risk assessment activities. The organization analyzes the operational environment in order to discern the likelihood of a cybersecurity event and the impact that the event could have on the organization. It is important that organizations identify emerging risks and use cyber threat information from internal and external sources to gain a better understanding of the likelihood and impact of cybersecurity events.

Step 5: Create a Target Profile. The organization creates a Target Profile that focuses on the assessment of the Framework Categories and Subcategories describing the organization's desired cybersecurity outcomes. Organizations also may develop their own additional Categories and

▓ NOTES

1. *See* 15 U.S.C. § 272(e)(1)(A)(i). The Cybersecurity Enhancement Act of 2014 (S.1353) became public law 113-274 on December 18, 2014 and may be found at: https://www.congress.gov/bill/113th-congress/senate-bill/1353/text.
2. *See* 15 U.S.C. § 272(e)(1)(A)(i). The Cybersecurity Enhancement Act of 2014 (S.1353) became public law 113-274 on December 18, 2014 and may be found at: https://www.congress.gov/bill/113th-congress/senate-bill/1353/text.
3. Executive Order no. 13636, *Improving Critical Infrastructure Cybersecurity*, DCPD-201300091, February 12, 2013. https://www.gpo.gov/fdsys/pkg/CFR-2014-title3-vol1/pdf/CFR-2014-title3-vol1-eo13636.pdf
4. The Department of Homeland Security (DHS) Critical Infrastructure program provides a listing of the sectors and their associated critical functions and value chains. http://www.dhs.gov/critical-infrastructure-sectors
5. See 42 U.S.C. § 5195c(e)). The U.S. Patriot Act of 2001 (H.R.3162) became public law 107 -56 on October 26, 2001 and may be found at: https://www.congress.gov/bill/107th-congress/house-bill/3162
6. International Organization for Standardization, *Risk management – Principles and guidelines*, ISO 31000:2009, 2009. http://www.iso.org/iso/home/standards/iso31000.htm
7. International Organization for Standardization/International Electrotechnical Commission, *Information technology – Security techniques – Information security risk management*, ISO/IEC 27005:2011, 2011. https://www.iso.org/standard/56742.html
8. Joint Task Force Transformation Initiative, *Managing Information Security Risk: Organization, Mission, and Information System View*, NIST Special Publication 800-39, March 2011. https://doi.org/10.6028/NIST.SP.800- 39
9. U.S. Department of Energy, *Electricity Subsector Cybersecurity Risk Management Process*, DOE/OE-0003, May 2012. https://energy.gov/sites/prod/files/Cybersecurity Risk Management Process Guideline - Final - May 2012.pdf
10. NIST Special Publication 800-160 Volume 1, *System Security Engineering, Considerations for a Multidisciplinary Approach in the Engineering of Trustworthy Secure Systems*, Ross et al, November 2016 (updated March 21, 2018), https://doi.org/10.6028/NIST.SP.800-160v1

Appendix B:
Risk Management:
ISO 31000*

W E LIVE IN AN ever-changing world where we are forced to deal with uncertainty every day. But how an organization tackles that uncertainty can be a key predictor of its success.

Risk is a necessary part of doing business, and in a world where enormous amounts of data are being processed at increasingly rapid rates, identifying and mitigating risks is a challenge for any company. It is no wonder then that many contracts and insurance agreements require solid evidence of good risk management practice. ISO 31000 provides direction on how companies can integrate risk-based decision making into an organization's governance, planning, management, reporting, policies, values and culture. It is an open, principles-based system, meaning it enables organizations to apply the principles in the standard to the organizational context.

 ## WHO IS ISO 31000 FOR?

ISO 31000 is applicable to all organizations, regardless of type, size, activities and location, and covers all types of risk. It was developed by a range of stakeholders and is intended for use by anyone who manages risks, not just professional risk managers.

 ## WHAT ARE THE BENEFITS FOR MY BUSINESS?

ISO 31000 helps organizations develop a risk management strategy to effectively identify and mitigate risks, thereby enhancing the likelihood of achieving

---

*This material is reprinted from https://www.iso.org/files/live/sites/isoorg/files/store/en/PUB100426.pdf

their objectives and increasing the protection of their assets. Its overarching goal is to develop a risk management culture where employees and stakeholders are aware of the importance of monitoring and managing risk. Implementing ISO 31000 also helps organizations see both the positive opportunities and negative consequences associated with risk, and allows for more informed, and thus more effective, decision making, namely in the allocation of resources. What's more, it can be an active component in improving an organization's governance and, ultimately, its performance.

WHY WAS IT *REVISED*?

All ISO standards are reviewed every five years and then revised if needed. This helps ensure they remain relevant, useful tools for the marketplace. A revised version of ISO 31000 was published in 2018 to take into account the evolution of the market and new challenges faced by business and organizations since the standard was first released in 2009. One example of this is the increased complexity of economic systems and emerging risk factors such as digital currency, both of which can present new and different types of risks to an organization on an international scale.

WHAT ARE THE MAIN DIFFERENCES?

ISO 31000:2018 provides more strategic guidance than ISO 31000:2009 and places more emphasis on both the involvement of senior management and the integration of risk management into the organization. This includes the recommendation to develop a statement or policy that confirms a commitment to risk management, assigning authority, responsibility and accountability at the appropriate levels within the organization and ensuring that the necessary resources are allocated to managing risk. The revised standard now also recommends that risk management be part of the organization's structure, processes, objectives, strategy and activities. It places a greater focus on creating value as the key driver of risk management and features other related principles such as continual improvement, the inclusion of stakeholders, being customized to the organization and consideration of human and cultural factors. The content has been streamlined to reflect an open systems model that regularly exchanges feedback with its external environment in order to fit a wider range of needs and contexts. The key objective is to make things clearer and easier, using plain language to define the fundamentals of risk management in a way that the reader will find easier to comprehend. The terminology is now more concise, with certain terms being moved to ISO Guide 73, *Risk management – Vocabulary*, which deals specifically with risk management terminology and is intended to be used alongside ISO 31000. Work has commenced on a terminology standard and implementation handbook to further enhance the understanding and applicability of the standard.

Who Was ISO 31000 Developed by?

ISO 31000 was developed by ISO's technical committee on risk management, ISO/TC 262. Other standards in its portfolio, which supports ISO 31000, include technical report ISO/TR 31004, *Risk management – Guidance for the implementation of ISO 31000*, and International Standard ISO/IEC 31010, *Risk management – Risk assessment techniques*, developed jointly with the International Electrotechnical Commission.

 ## WHAT ABOUT CERTIFICATION?

ISO 31000 provides guidelines, not requirements, and is therefore not intended for certification purposes.

 ## HOW DO I GET STARTED?

- Be aware of your organization's key objectives – this will help you clarify the targets and requirements of your risk management system.
- Assess your current governance structure – this will ensure you allocate the right roles, responsibilities and reporting procedures when it comes to risk.
- Define your level of commitment – what resources will you be able to allocate to implementing or maintaining a risk management system.

 ## ABOUT ISO

ISO (International Organization for Standardization) is an independent, non-governmental organization with a membership of 162* national standards bodies. Through its members, ISO brings together experts to share knowledge

---

*February 2018.

and develop voluntary, consensus-based, market-relevant International Standards that support innovation and provide solutions to global challenges. ISO has published more than 22 000* International Standards and related documents covering almost every industry, from technology to food safety, to agriculture and healthcare. For more information, please visit: www.iso.org.

---

*February 2018.

Appendix C: Privacy by Design The 7 Foundational Principles Implementation and Mapping of Fair Information Practices*

ANN CAVOUKIAN, PH.D.
Information & Privacy Commissioner, Ontario, Canada

PURPOSE:

This document provides readers with additional information, clarification and guidance on applying the 7 Foundational Principles of *Privacy by Design (PbD)*.

This guidance is intended to serve as a reference framework and may be used for developing more detailed criteria for application and audit/verification purposes.

SCOPE:

These information management principles – and the philosophy and methodology they express – can apply to specific technologies, business operations, physical architectures and networked infrastructure, and even to entire information ecosystems and governance models.

The universal principles of the Fair Information Practices (FIPs) are affirmed by those of *Privacy by Design*, but go beyond them to seek the highest global standard possible. Extending beyond FIPs, *PbD* represents a significant "raising" of the bar in the area of privacy protection.

CONTEXT:

With the shift from industrial manufacturing to knowledge creation and service delivery, the value of information and the need to manage it responsibly

---

*This material is reprinted from https://iab.org/wp-content/IAB-uploads/2011/03/fred_carter.pdf

have grown dramatically. At the same time, rapid innovation, global competition and increasing system complexity present profound challenges for informational privacy.

While we would like to enjoy the benefits of innovation – new conveniences and efficiencies – we must also preserve our freedom of choice and personal control over our data flows. Always a social norm, privacy has nonetheless evolved over the years, beyond being viewed solely as a legal compliance requirement, to also being recognized as a market imperative and critical enabler of trust and freedoms in our present-day information society.

There is a growing understanding that innovation, creativity and competitiveness must be approached from a "design-thinking" perspective – namely, a way of viewing the world and overcoming constraints that is at once holistic, interdisciplinary, integrative, innovative, and inspiring.

Privacy, too, must be approached from the same design-thinking perspective. Privacy must be incorporated into networked data systems and technologies, **by default**. Privacy must become integral to organizational priorities, project objectives, design processes, and planning operations. Privacy must be embedded into every standard, protocol and process that touches our lives. This document seeks to make this possible by striving to establish a universal framework for the strongest protection of privacy available in the modern era.

The 7 Foundational Principles of Privacy by Design are presented below *in Bold*, followed by the FIPs principles that map onto each one.

1. *PROACTIVE* NOT REACTIVE; *PREVENTATIVE* NOT REMEDIAL

The Privacy by Design approach is characterized by proactive rather than reactive measures. It anticipates and prevents privacy invasive events before they happen. PbD does not wait for privacy risks to materialize, nor does it offer remedies for resolving privacy infractions once they have occurred – it aims to prevent them from occurring. In short, Privacy by Design comes before-the-fact, not after.

Whether applied to information technologies, organizational practices, physical design, or networked information ecosystems, *PbD* begins with an explicit recognition of the value and benefits of proactively adopting strong privacy practices, early and consistently (for example, preventing (internal) data breaches from happening in the first place). This implies:

- A clear commitment, at the highest levels, to set and enforce high standards of privacy – generally higher than the standards set out by global laws and regulation.
- A privacy commitment that is demonstrably shared throughout by user communities and stakeholders, in a culture of continuous improvement.
- Established methods to recognize poor privacy designs, anticipate poor privacy practices and outcomes, and correct any negative impacts, well before they occur in proactive, systematic, and innovative ways.

2. PRIVACY AS THE *DEFAULT*

We can all be certain of one thing – the default rules! Privacy by Design seeks to deliver the maximum degree of privacy by ensuring that personal data are automatically protected in any given IT system or business practice. If an individual does nothing, their privacy still remains intact. No action is required on the part of the individual to protect their privacy – it is built into the system, by default.

This *PbD* principle, which could be viewed as **Privacy by Default**, is particularly informed by the following FIPs:

- **Purpose Specification** – the purposes for which personal information is collected, used, retained and disclosed shall be communicated to the individual (data subject) at or before the time the information is collected. Specified purposes should be clear, limited and relevant to the circumstances.
- **Collection Limitation** – the collection of personal information must be fair, lawful and limited to that which is necessary for the specified purposes.
- **Data Minimization** – the collection of personally identifiable information should be kept to a strict minimum. The design of programs, information and communications technologies, and systems should begin with non-identifiable interactions and transactions, as the default. Wherever possible, identifiability, observability, and linkability of personal information should be minimized.

▦ **Use, Retention, and Disclosure Limitation** – the use, retention, and disclosure of personal information shall be limited to the relevant purposes identified to the individual, for which he or she has consented, except where otherwise required by law. Personal information shall be retained only as long as necessary to fulfill the stated purposes, and then securely destroyed.

Where the need or use of personal information is not clear, there shall be a presumption of privacy and the precautionary principle shall apply: the default settings shall be the most privacy protective.

3. PRIVACY *EMBEDDED* INTO DESIGN

Privacy by Design is embedded into the design and architecture of IT systems and business practices. It is not bolted on as an add-on, after the fact. The result is that privacy becomes an essential component of the core functionality being delivered. Privacy is integral to the system, without diminishing functionality.

Privacy must be embedded into technologies, operations, and information architectures in a holistic, integrative and creative way. Holistic, because additional, broader contexts must always be considered. Integrative, because all stakeholders and interests should be consulted. Creative, because embedding privacy sometimes means re-inventing existing choices because the alternatives are unacceptable.

▦ A systemic, principled approach to embedding privacy should be adopted – one that relies upon accepted standards and frameworks, which are amenable to external reviews and audits. All fair information practices should be applied with equal rigour, at every step in the design and operation.

▦ Wherever possible, detailed privacy impact and risk assessments should be carried out and published, clearly documenting the privacy risks and all measures taken to mitigate those risks, including consideration of alternatives and the selection of metrics.

▪ The privacy impacts of the resulting technology, operation or information architecture, and their uses, should be demonstrably minimized, and not easily degraded through use, misconfiguration or error.

4. FULL FUNCTIONALITY – POSITIVE-SUM, NOT ZERO-SUM

Privacy by Design seeks to accommodate all legitimate interests and objectives in a positive-sum "win- win" manner, not through a dated, zero-sum approach, where unnecessary trade-offs are made. Privacy by Design avoids the pretence of false dichotomies, such as privacy vs. security, demonstrating that it is possible, and far more desirable, to have both.

Privacy by Design does not simply involve the making of declarations and commitments – it relates to satisfying all legitimate objectives – not only the privacy goals. *Privacy by Design* is doubly-enabling in nature, permitting full functionality – real, practical results and beneficial outcomes to be achieved for multiple parties.

▪ When embedding privacy into a given technology, process, or system, it should be done in such a way that full functionality is not impaired, and to the greatest extent possible, that all requirements are optimized.
▪ Privacy is often positioned in a zero-sum manner as having to compete with other legitimate interests, design objectives, and technical capabilities, in a given domain. *Privacy by Design* rejects taking such an approach – it embraces legitimate non-privacy objectives and accommodates them, in an innovative positive-sum manner.
▪ All interests and objectives must be clearly documented, desired functions articulated, metrics agreed upon and applied, and trade-offs rejected as often being unnecessary, in favour of finding a solution that enables multi-functionality.

Additional recognition is garnered for creativity and innovation in achieving all objectives and functionalities in an integrative, positive-sum manner. Entities that succeed in overcoming outmoded zero-sum choices are demonstrating first-class global privacy leadership, having achieved the Gold Standard.

5. END-TO-END SECURITY – LIFECYCLE PROTECTION

Privacy by Design, having been embedded into the system prior to the first element of information being collected, extends securely throughout the entire lifecycle of the data involved — strong security measures are essential to privacy, from start to finish. This ensures that all data are securely retained, and then securely destroyed at the end of the process, in a timely fashion. Thus, Privacy by Design ensures cradle to grave, secure lifecycle management of information, end-to-end.

Privacy must be continuously protected across the entire domain and throughout the life-cycle of the data in question. There should be no gaps in either protection or accountability. The "Security" principle has special relevance here because, at its essence, without strong security, there can be no privacy.

- ▪ **Security** – Entities must assume responsibility for the security of personal information (generally commensurate with the degree of sensitivity) throughout its entire lifecycle, consistent with standards that have been developed by recognized standards development bodies.
- ▪ **Applied security** standards must assure the confidentiality, integrity and availability of personal data throughout its lifecycle including, *inter alia*, methods of secure destruction, appropriate encryption, and strong access control and logging methods.

6. VISIBILITY AND TRANSPARENCY

Privacy by Design seeks to assure all stakeholders that whatever the business practice or technology involved, it is in fact, operating according to the stated promises and objectives, subject to independent verification. Its component parts and operations remain visible and transparent, to both users and providers alike. Remember, trust but verify!

Visibility and transparency are essential to establishing accountability and trust. This PbD principle tracks well to Fair Information Practices in their entirety, but for auditing purposes, special emphasis may be placed upon the following FIPs:

▦ **Accountabilty** – The collection of personal information entails a duty of care for its protection. Responsibility for all privacy-related policies and procedures shall be documented and communicated as appropriate, and assigned to a specified individual. When transferring personal information to third parties, equivalent privacy protection through contractual or other means shall be secured.
▦ **Openness** – Openness and transparency are key to accountability. Information about the policies and practices relating to the management of personal information shall be made readily available to individuals.
▦ **Compliance** – Complaint and redress mechanisms should be established, and information communicated about them to individuals, including how to access the next level of appeal. Necessary steps to monitor, evaluate, and verify compliance with privacy policies and procedures should be taken.

7. RESPECT FOR USER PRIVACY

Above all, Privacy by Design requires architects and operators to keep the interests of the individual uppermost by offering such measures as strong privacy defaults, appropriate notice, and empowering user-friendly options. Keep it user-centric!

The best *Privacy by Design* results are usually those that are consciously designed around the interests and needs of individual users, who have the greatest vested interest in the management of their own personal data.

Empowering data subjects to play an active role in the management of their own data may be the single most effective check against abuses and misuses of privacy and personal data. Respect for User Privacy is supported by the following FIPs:

▦ **Consent** – The individual's free and specific consent is required for the collection, use or disclosure of personal information, except where otherwise permitted by law. The greater the sensitivity of the data, the clearer and more specific the quality of the consent required. Consent may be withdrawn at a later date.

■ **Accuracy** – personal information shall be as accurate, complete, and up-to-date as is necessary to fulfill the specified purposes.

■ **Access** – Individuals shall be provided access to their personal information and informed of its uses and disclosures. Individuals shall be able to challenge the accuracy and completeness of the information and have it amended as appropriate.

■ **Compliance** – Organizations must establish complaint and redress mechanisms, and communicate information about them to the public, including how to access the next level of appeal.

Respect for User Privacy goes beyond these FIPs, and extends to the need for human-machine interfaces to be human-centered, user-centric and user-friendly so that informed privacy decisions may be reliably exercised. Similarly, business operations and physical architectures should also demonstrate the same degree of consideration for the individual, who should feature prominently at the centre of operations involving collections of personal data.

+++

Further information and all references at: www.privacybydesign.ca

Appendix D: KnowBe4 – Free IT Security Tools

THE TACTICS OF THREAT actors are constantly changing, making it difficult for any organization with relatively few employees to stay up-to-date on the latest threats. As discussed in Chapter 4, "Cyber Culture," humans are complex, and we often decide based on how we feel. That irrationality can be beneficial in terms of cybersecurity. Employees can detect potentially malicious activity or attempts as the first line of defense because "it just doesn't feel right." We want to use that irrationality vs. judgment—that "gut feeling"—to our advantage for business protection. As a result, cyber culture is critical. Cyber culture cannot be imposed; written policies and processes can help to support and protect culture, but they cannot create it. Cyber culture cannot be completely controlled because culture lives in the hearts and minds of employees. The common underlying issue for start-ups and small- and medium-sized businesses appears to be management commitment, which drives budgeting, resource allocation, and effective cybersecurity implementation. Cybersecurity is not just an issue for IT or cybersecurity teams to discuss; it should be on the agenda of all founder and executive meetings of every start-up or SMB.

Below is the list of KnowBe4 free tools for startups and SMBs that can be found at https://www.knowbe4.com/free-it-security-tools.

KNOWBE4—FREE IT SECURITY TOOLS

- Featured Tool: Browser Password Inspector

PHISHING TOOLS

- Phishing Security Test
- Phishing Reply Test
- Social Media Phishing Test
- Phish Alert Button
- Second Chance

 SECURITY AWARENESS TRAINING TOOLS

- Automated Security Awareness Program (ASAP)
- Training Preview

 PASSWORD TOOLS

- Weak Password Test
- Browser Password Inspector
- Password Exposure Test
- Multi-Factor Authentication Security Assessment

 EMAIL SECURITY TOOLS

- Email Exposure Check Pro
- Domain Spoof Test
- Mailserver Assessment (MSA)
- Domain Doppelgänger

 MALWARE TOOLS

- Ransomware Simulator Tool
- USB Security Test

 COMPLIANCE TOOLS

- Compliance Audit Readiness Assessment

Appendix E: Cyber Resilience Framework by NIST[1]

A S ALREADY OUTLINED IN Chapter 5, Appendix E is for further reading and guidance on cyber resilience. A robust cyber resilience strategy empowers executives to foresee a compromise and decide what is and is not a priority. A governance structure, complete with policies and processes, may be integrated into business strategy. The key is always to have an organization-specific cyber resilience framework regularly evaluated to ensure that it remains relevant in the face of emerging challenges. Below are the two chapters of NIST SP 800-160 Vol. by the U.S. Department of Homeland Security 2.

 CHAPTER TWO

The Fundamentals

Understanding the Concepts Associated with Cyber Resiliency

This section presents an engineering framework for understanding and applying cyber resiliency, the cyber resiliency constructs that are part of the framework, a concept of use for the framework, and engineering considerations for implementing cyber resiliency in the system life cycle. The discussion relies on several terms including cyber resiliency concepts and constructs, engineering practices, and solutions.

---

[1]Ron Ross et al., 2021/NIST/Public domain

Cyber resiliency *concepts* are related to the problem domain and the solution set for cyber resiliency. The concepts are represented in cyber resiliency risk models and by cyber resiliency constructs.[19] The *constructs* are the basic elements (i.e., building blocks) of the cyber resiliency engineering framework and include goals, objectives, techniques, implementation approaches, and design principles.[20] The framework provides a way to understand the cyber resiliency problem and solution domain. Cyber resiliency goals and objectives identify the "what" of cyber resiliency—that is, what properties and behaviors are integral to cyber-resilient systems. Cyber resiliency techniques, implementation approaches, and design principles characterize the ways of achieving or improving resilience in the face of threats to systems and system components (i.e., the "how" of cyber resiliency). Cyber resiliency constructs address both adversarial and non-adversarial threats from cyber and non-cyber sources.

Cyber resiliency *engineering practices* are the methods, processes, modeling, and analytical techniques used to identify and analyze proposed solutions. The application of these practices in system life cycle processes ensures that cyber resiliency *solutions* are driven by stakeholder requirements and protection needs, which, in turn, guide and inform the development of system requirements for the system of interest [ISO 15288, SP 800-160 v1]. Such solutions consist of combinations of technologies, architectural decisions, systems engineering processes, and operational policies, processes, procedures, or practices that solve problems in the cyber resiliency domain. They provide a sufficient level of cyber resiliency to meet stakeholder needs and reduce risks to organizational mission or business capabilities in the presence of a variety of threat sources, including the APT.

Cyber resiliency *solutions* use cyber resiliency techniques and approaches to implementing those techniques, as described in Section 2.1.3. Cyber resiliency solutions apply the design principles described in Section 2.1.4 and implement mechanisms (e.g., controls and control enhancements defined in [SP 800-53]) that apply one or more cyber resiliency techniques or implementation approaches or that are intended to achieve one or more cyber resiliency objectives. These mechanisms are selected in response to the security and cyber resiliency requirements defined as part of the system life cycle and requirements

---

[19]As discussed in Section D.1, cyber resiliency concepts and constructs are informed by definitions and frameworks related to other forms of resilience as well as system survivability. A reader unfamiliar with the concept of resilience may benefit from reading that appendix before this section.
[20]Additional constructs (e.g., sub-objectives, capabilities) may be used in some modeling and analytic practices.

engineering process described in [SP 800-160 v1] or to mitigate security and cyber resiliency risks that arise from architectural or design decisions.

2.1 CYBER RESILIENCY ENGINEERING FRAMEWORK

The following sections provide a description of the framework for cyber resiliency engineering.[21] The framework constructs include cyber resiliency goals, objectives, techniques, implementation approaches, and design principles. The relationship among constructs is also described. These constructs, like cyber resiliency, can be applied at levels beyond the system (e.g., mission or business function level, organizational level, or sector level). Table 1 summarizes the definition and purpose of each construct, and how each construct is applied at the system level.

TABLE 1 Cyber Resiliency Constructs

Construct	Definition, Purpose, and Application at the System Level
GOAL	A high-level statement supporting (or focusing on) one aspect (i.e., anticipate, withstand, recover, adapt) in the definition of cyber resiliency.
	Purpose: Align the definition of cyber resiliency with definitions of other types of resilience.
	Application: Can be used to express high-level stakeholder concerns, goals, or priorities.
OBJECTIVE	A high-level statement (designed to be restated in system-specific and stakeholder-specific terms) of what a system must achieve in its operational environment and throughout its life cycle to meet stakeholder needs for mission assurance and resilient security. The objectives are more specific than goals and more relatable to threats.
	Purpose: Enable stakeholders and systems engineers to reach a common understanding of cyber resiliency concerns and priorities; facilitate the definition of metrics or measures of effectiveness (MOEs).
	Application: Used in scoring methods or summaries of analyses (e.g., cyber resiliency posture assessments).

(continued)

---

[21]The cyber resiliency engineering framework described in this publication is based on and consistent with the *Cyber Resiliency Engineering Framework* developed by The MITRE Corporation [Bodeau11].

TABLE 1   Cyber Resiliency Constructs (*Continued*)

Construct	Definition, Purpose, and Application at the System Level
Sub-Objective	A statement, subsidiary to a cyber resiliency objective, that emphasizes different aspects of that objective or identifies methods to achieve that objective. Purpose: Serve as a step in the hierarchical refinement of an objective into activities or capabilities for which performance measures can be defined. Application: Used in scoring methods or analyses; may be reflected in system functional requirements.
Activity or Capability	A statement of a capability or action that supports the achievement of a sub-objective and, hence, an objective. Purpose: Facilitate the definition of metrics or MOEs. While a representative set of activities or capabilities have been identified in [Bodeau18b], these are intended solely as a starting point for selection, tailoring, and prioritization. Application: Used in scoring methods or analyses; reflected in system functional requirements.
STRATEGIC DESIGN PRINCIPLE	A high-level statement that reflects an aspect of the risk management strategy that informs systems security engineering practices for an organization, mission, or system. Purpose: Guide and inform engineering analyses and risk analyses throughout the system life cycle. Highlight different structural design principles, cyber resiliency techniques, and implementation approaches. Application: Included, cited, or restated in system non-functional requirements (e.g., requirements in a Statement of Work [SOW] for analyses or documentation).
STRUCTURAL DESIGN PRINCIPLE	A statement that captures experience in defining system architectures and designs. Purpose: Guide and inform design and implementation decisions throughout the system life cycle. Highlight different cyber resiliency techniques and implementation approaches. Application: Included, cited, or restated in system non-functional requirements (e.g., Statement of Work [SOW] requirements for analyses or documentation); used in systems engineering to guide the use of techniques, implementation approaches, technologies, and practices.

Construct	Definition, Purpose, and Application at the System Level
TECHNIQUE	A set or class of technologies, processes, or practices providing capabilities to achieve one or more cyber resiliency objectives.
	Purpose: Characterize technologies, practices, products, controls, or requirements so that their contribution to cyber resiliency can be understood.
	Application: Used in engineering analysis to screen technologies, practices, products, controls, solutions, or requirements; used in the system by implementing or integrating technologies, practices, products, or solutions.
IMPLEMENTA-TION APPROACH	A subset of the technologies and processes of a cyber resiliency technique defined by how the capabilities are implemented.
	Purpose: Characterize technologies, practices, products, controls, or requirements so that their contribution to cyber resiliency and their potential effects on threat events can be understood.
	Application: Used in engineering analysis to screen technologies, practices, products, controls, solutions, or requirements; used in the system by implementing or integrating technologies, practices, products, or solutions.
SOLUTION	A combination of technologies, architectural decisions, systems engineering processes, and operational processes, procedures, or practices that solves a problem in the cyber resiliency domain.
	Purpose: Provide a sufficient level of cyber resiliency to meet stakeholder needs and reduce risks to mission or business capabilities in the presence of advanced persistent threats.
	Application: Integrated into the system or its operational environment.
MITIGATION	An action or practice using a technology, control, solution, or a set of these that reduces the level of risk associated with a threat event or threat scenario.
	Purpose: Characterize actions, practices, approaches, controls, solutions, or combinations of these in terms of their potential effects on threat events, threat scenarios, or risks.
	Application: Integrated into the system as it is used.

2.1.1 Cyber Resiliency Goals

Cyber resiliency, like security, is a concern at multiple levels in an organization. The four cyber resiliency goals, which are common to many resilience definitions, are included in the definition and the cyber resiliency engineering framework to provide linkage between risk management decisions at the system level, the mission and business process level, and the organizational level. Organizational risk management strategies can use cyber resiliency goals and associated strategies to incorporate cyber resiliency.[22]

For cyber resiliency engineering analysis, cyber resiliency objectives rather than goals are the starting point. The term *adversity*, as used in the cyber resiliency goals in Table 2, includes stealthy, persistent, sophisticated, and well-resourced adversaries (i.e., the APT) who may have compromised system components and established a foothold within an organization's systems.

TABLE 2 Cyber Resiliency Goals

Goal	Description
ANTICIPATE	Maintain a state of informed preparedness for adversity.
	Discussion: Adversity refers to adverse conditions, stresses, attacks, or compromises on cyber resources. Adverse conditions can include natural disasters and structural failures (e.g., power failures). Stresses can include unexpectedly high-performance loads. Adversity can be caused or taken advantage of by an APT actor. Informed preparedness involves contingency planning, including plans for mitigating and investigating threat events as well as for responding to discoveries of vulnerabilities or supply chain compromises. Cyber threat intelligence (CTI) provides vital information for informed preparedness.
WITHSTAND	Continue essential mission or business functions despite adversity.
	Discussion: Detection is not required for this goal to be meaningful and achievable. An APT actor's activities may be undetected, or they may be detected but incorrectly attributed to user error or other stresses. The identification of essential organizational missions or business functions is necessary to achieve this goal. In addition, supporting processes, systems, services, networks, and infrastructures must also be identified. The criticality of resources and capabilities of essential functions can vary over time.

---

[22] See Appendix C.

Goal	Description
RECOVER	Restore mission or business functions during and after adversity.
	Discussion: The restoration of functions and data can be incremental. A key challenge is determining how much trust can be placed in restored functions and data as restoration progresses. Other threat events or conditions in the operational or technical environment can interfere with recovery, and an APT actor may seek to take advantage of confusion about recovery processes to establish a new foothold in the organization's systems.
ADAPT	Modify mission or business functions and/or supporting capabilities in response to predicted changes in the technical, operational, or threat environments.
	Discussion: Change can occur at different scales and over different time frames, so tactical and strategic adaption may be needed. Modification can be applied to processes and procedures as well as technology. Changes in the technical environment can include emerging technologies (e.g., artificial intelligence, 5th generation mobile network [5G], Internet of Things) and the retirement of obsolete products. Changes in the operational environment of the organization can result from regulatory or policy changes, as well as the introduction of new business processes or workflows. Analyses of such changes and of interactions between changes can reveal how these could modify the attack surface or introduce fragility.

2.1.2 Cyber Resiliency Objectives

Cyber resiliency *objectives*[23] are specific statements of what a system is intended to achieve in its operational environment and throughout its life cycle to meet stakeholder needs for mission assurance and resilient security. Cyber resiliency objectives, as described in Table 3, support interpretation,[24] facilitate prioritization and assessment, and enable development of questions such as:

---

[23]The term *objective* is defined and used in multiple ways. In this document, uses are qualified (e.g., cyber resiliency objectives, security objectives [FIPS 199], adversary objectives [MITRE18], engineering objectives or purposes [ISO 24765]) for clarity.

[24]Cyber resiliency goals and objectives can be viewed as two levels of fundamental objectives, as used in Decision Theory [Clemen13]. Alternately, cyber resiliency goals can be viewed as fundamental objectives and cyber resiliency objectives as enabling objectives [Brtis16]. By contrast, cyber resiliency techniques can be viewed as means objectives [Clemen13].

TABLE 3 Cyber Resiliency Objectives[25]

Objective	Description
PREVENT OR AVOID	Preclude the successful execution of an attack or the realization of adverse conditions.
	Discussion: This objective relates to an organization's preferences for different risk response approaches. Risk avoidance or threat avoidance is one possible risk response approach and is feasible under restricted circumstances. Preventing a threat event from occurring is another possible risk response, similarly feasible under restricted circumstances.
PREPARE	Maintain a set of realistic courses of action that address predicted or anticipated adversity.
	Discussion: This objective is driven by the recognition that adversity will occur. It specifically relates to an organization's contingency planning, continuity of operations plan (COOP), training, exercises, and incident response and recovery plans for critical systems and infrastructures.
CONTINUE	Maximize the duration and viability of essential mission or business functions during adversity.
	Discussion: This objective specifically relates to essential functions. Its assessment is aligned with the definition of performance parameters, analysis of functional dependencies, and identification of critical assets. Note that shared services and common infrastructures, while not identified as essential per se, may be necessary to essential functions and, thus, related to this objective.
CONSTRAIN	Limit damage[26] from adversity.
	Discussion: This objective specifically applies to critical or high-value assets—those cyber assets that contain or process sensitive information, are mission-essential, or provide infrastructure services to mission-essential capabilities.

---

[25]See Appendix D for specific relationships between objectives and goals.
[26]From the perspective of cyber resiliency, *damage* can be to the organization (e.g., loss of reputation, increased existential risk), missions or business functions (e.g., decrease in the ability to complete the current mission and to accomplish future missions), security (e.g., decrease in the ability to achieve the security objectives of integrity, availability, and confidentiality or decrease in the ability to prevent, detect, and respond to cyber incidents), the system (e.g., decrease in the ability to meet system requirements or unauthorized use of system resources), or specific system elements (e.g., physical destruction; corruption, modification, or fabrication of information).

Objective	Description
RECONSTITUTE	Restore as much mission or business functionality as possible after adversity. Discussion: This objective relates to essential functions, critical assets, and the services and infrastructures on which they depend. A key aspect of achieving this objective is ensuring that recovery, restoration, or reconstitution efforts result in trustworthy resources. This objective is not predicated on analysis of the source of adversity (e.g., attribution) and can be achieved even without detection of adversity via ongoing efforts to ensure the timely and correct availability of resources.
UNDERSTAND	Maintain useful representations of mission and business dependencies and the status of resources with respect to possible adversity. **Discussion:** This objective supports the achievement of all other objectives, most notably Prepare, Reconstitute, Transform, and Re-Architect. An organization's plans for continuous diagnostics and mitigation (CDM), infrastructure services, and other services support this objective. The detection of anomalies, particularly suspicious or unexpected events or conditions, also supports achieving this objective. However, this objective includes understanding resource dependencies and status independent of detection. This objective also relates to an organization's use of forensics and cyber threat intelligence information sharing.
TRANSFORM	Modify mission or business functions and supporting processes to handle adversity and address environmental changes more effectively. **Discussion:** This objective specifically applies to workflows for essential functions, supporting processes, and incident response and recovery plans for critical assets and essential functions. Tactical modifications are usually procedural or configuration-related; longer-term modifications can involve restructuring operational processes or governance responsibilities while leaving the underlying technical architecture unchanged.
RE-ARCHITECT	Modify architectures to handle adversity and address environmental changes more effectively. **Discussion:** This objective specifically applies to system architectures and mission architectures, which include the technical architecture of the system-of-systems supporting a mission or business function. In addition, this objective applies to architectures for critical infrastructures and services, which frequently support multiple essential functions.

▩ What does each cyber resiliency objective mean in the context of the organization and the mission or business process that the system is intended to support?

▩ Which cyber resiliency objectives are most important to a given stakeholder?

▩ To what degree can each cyber resiliency objective be achieved?

▩ How quickly and cost-effectively can each cyber resiliency objective be achieved?

▩ With what degree of confidence or trust can each cyber resiliency objective be achieved?

Because stakeholders may find the cyber resiliency objectives difficult to relate to their specific concerns, the objectives can be tailored to reflect the organization's missions and business functions or operational concept for the system of interest. Tailoring the cyber resiliency objectives can also help stakeholders determine which objectives apply and the priority to assign to each objective. Cyber resiliency objectives can be hierarchically refined to emphasize the different aspects of an objective or the methods to achieve an objective, thus creating sub- objectives.[27] Cyber resiliency objectives (and sub-objectives as needed to help stakeholders interpret the objectives for their concerns) enable stakeholders to assert their different resiliency priorities based on organizational missions or business functions.

2.1.3 Cyber Resiliency Techniques and Approaches

Cyber resiliency goals and objectives provide a vocabulary for describing what properties and capabilities are needed. Cyber resiliency techniques, approaches, and design principles (discussed in Section 2.1.4) provide a vocabulary for discussing how a system can achieve its cyber resiliency goals and objectives. A cyber resiliency technique is a set or class of practices and technologies intended to achieve one or more goals or objectives by providing capabilities.

The following 14 techniques are part of the cyber resiliency engineering framework:

1. **Adaptive Response:** Implement agile courses of action to manage risks.
2. **Analytic Monitoring:** Monitor and analyze a wide range of properties and behaviors on an ongoing basis and in a coordinated way.

---

[27]Table D-1 in Appendix D provides representative examples of sub-objectives.

3. **Contextual Awareness:** Construct and maintain current representations of the posture of missions or business functions while considering threat events and courses of action.
4. **Coordinated Protection:** Ensure that protection mechanisms operate in a coordinated and effective manner.
5. **Deception:** Mislead, confuse, hide critical assets from, or expose covertly tainted assets to the adversary.
6. **Diversity:** Use heterogeneity to minimize common mode failures, particularly threat events exploiting common vulnerabilities.
7. **Dynamic Positioning:** Distribute and dynamically relocate functionality or system resources.
8. **Non-Persistence:** Generate and retain resources as needed or for a limited time.
9. **Privilege Restriction:** Restrict privileges based on attributes of users and system elements, as well as on environmental factors.
10. **Realignment:** Structure systems and resource uses to align with mission or business function needs, reduce current and anticipated risks, and accommodate the evolution of technical, operational, and threat environments.
11. **Redundancy:** Provide multiple protected instances of critical resources.
12. **Segmentation:** Define and separate system elements based on criticality and trustworthiness.
13. **Substantiated Integrity:** Ascertain whether critical system elements have been corrupted.
14. **Unpredictability:** Make changes randomly or unpredictably.

The cyber resiliency techniques are described in Appendix D. Each technique is characterized by both the capabilities it provides and the intended consequences of using the technologies or the processes it includes. The cyber resiliency techniques reflect an understanding of the threats as well as the technologies, processes, and concepts related to improving cyber resiliency to address the threats. The cyber resiliency engineering framework assumes the cyber resiliency techniques will be selectively applied to the architecture or design of organizational mission or business functions and their supporting system resources. Since natural synergies and conflicts exist among the cyber resiliency techniques, system engineering trade-offs must be made. Cyber resiliency techniques are expected to change over time as threats evolve, technology advances are made based on research, security practices evolve, and new ideas emerge.

Twelve of the 14 cyber resiliency techniques can be applied to adversarial or non-adversarial threats (including cyber-related and non-cyber-related threats). The cyber resiliency techniques specific to adversarial threats are Deception and Unpredictability. Cyber resiliency techniques are also interdependent. For example, the Analytic Monitoring technique supports Contextual Awareness. The Unpredictability technique, however, is different from the other techniques in that it is always applied in conjunction with some other technique (e.g., working with the Dynamic Positioning technique to establish unpredictable times for repositioning potential targets of interest). The definitions of cyber resiliency techniques are intentionally broad to insulate the definitions from changing technologies and threats, thus limiting the need for frequent changes to the set of techniques.

To support engineering analysis, multiple representative approaches to implementing each technique are identified. As illustrated in Figure 1, an *implementation approach* (or, for brevity, an *approach*) is a subset of the technologies and processes included in a technique that are defined by how the capabilities are implemented or how the intended outcomes are achieved.

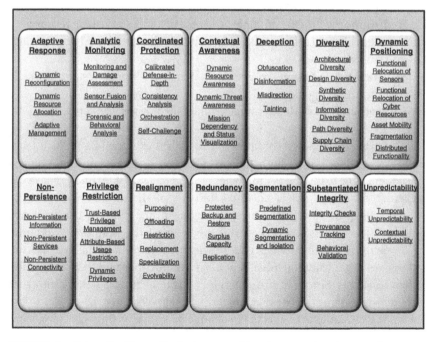

FIGURE 1   Cyber Resiliency Techniques and Implementation Approaches

Table D-4 in Appendix D defines representative approaches and gives representative examples of technologies and practices. The set of approaches for a specific technique is not exhaustive and represents relatively mature technologies and practices. Thus, technologies emerging from research can be characterized in terms of the techniques they apply while not being covered by any of the representative approaches.[28]

Non-Persistence	Privilege Restriction	Realign-ment	Redundancy	Segmen-tation	Substantiated Integrity	Unpredict-ability

2.1.4 Cyber Resiliency Design Principles

Systems engineers and architects use *design principles*[29] as guidance in design decisions and analysis. A design principle takes the form of a terse statement or a phrase identifying a key concept accompanied by one or more statements that describe how that concept applies to system design (where "system" is broadly construed to include operational processes and procedures and may also include development and maintenance environments) [Bodeau17]. Design principles are defined for many specialty engineering disciplines using the terminology, experience, and research results that are specific to the specialty.

Cyber resiliency design principles, like those from other specialty disciplines, can be applied in different ways at multiple stages in the system life cycle, including the operations and maintenance stage. The design principles can also be used in a variety of system development models, including agile and spiral development. The cyber resiliency design principles identified in this publication can serve as a starting point for systems engineers and architects. For any given situation, only a subset of the design principles is selected, and those principles are tailored or "re-expressed" in terms more meaningful to the program, system, or system-of- systems to which they apply.

The cyber resiliency design principles are strongly informed by and can be aligned with design principles from other specialty disciplines, such as the security design principles in [SP 800-160 v1]. Many of the cyber resiliency design principles are based on design principles for security, resilience engineering, or both. Design principles can be characterized as *strategic*

---

[28]Decisions about whether and how to apply less mature technologies and practices are strongly influenced by the organization's risk management strategy. See [SP 800-39].

[29]As described in [Bodeau17], a design principle refers to distillations of experience designing, implementing, integrating, and upgrading systems.

(i.e., applied throughout the systems engineering process, guiding the direction of engineering analyses) or *structural* (i.e., directly affecting the architecture and design of the system or system elements) [Ricci14]. Both strategic and structural cyber resiliency design principles can be reflected in security-related systems engineering artifacts. A complete list of strategic and structural cyber resiliency design principles is provided in Appendix D.

2.1.5 Relationship Among Cyber Resiliency Constructs

Cyber resiliency constructs, including goals, objectives, techniques, implementation approaches, and design principles, enable systems engineers to express cyber resiliency concepts and the relationships among them. The cyber resiliency constructs also relate to risk management. That relationship leads systems engineers to analyze cyber resiliency solutions in terms of potential effects on risk and on specific threat events or types of malicious cyber activities. The selection and relative priority of these cyber resiliency constructs is determined by the organization's strategy for managing the risks of depending on systems, which include cyber resources—in particular, by the organization's *risk framing*.[30] The relative priority of the cyber resiliency goals and objectives and relevance of the cyber resiliency design principles are determined by the risk management strategy of the organization, which takes into consideration the concerns of, constraints on, and equities of all stakeholders (including those who are not part of the organization). Figure 2 illustrates the relationships among the cyber resiliency constructs. These relationships are represented by mapping tables in Appendix D. As Figure 2 illustrates, a cyber-resilient system is the result of the engineering selection, prioritization, and application of cyber resiliency design principles, techniques, and implementation approaches. The risk management strategy for the organization is translated into specific interpretations and prioritizations of cyber resiliency goals and objectives, which guide and inform trade-offs among different forms of risk mitigation.

---

[30]The first component of risk management addresses how organizations *frame* risk or establish a risk context—that is, describing the environment in which risk-based decisions are made. The purpose of the risk-framing component is to produce a *risk management strategy* that addresses how organizations intend to assess risk, respond to risk, and monitor risk—making explicit and transparent the risk perceptions that organizations routinely use in making both investment and operational decisions [SP 800-39]. The risk management strategy addresses how the organization manages the risks of depending on systems that include cyber resources; is part of a comprehensive, enterprise-wide risk management strategy; and reflects stakeholder concerns and priorities.

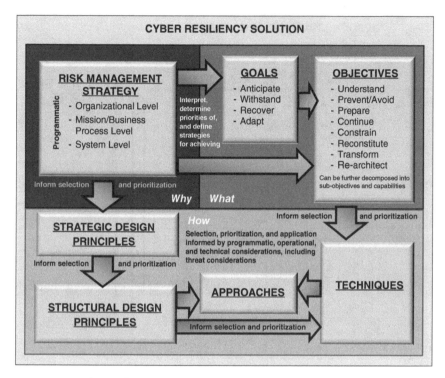

FIGURE 2   Relationships Among Cyber Resiliency Constructs

 ## 2.2 CYBER RESILIENCY IN THE SYSTEM LIFE CYCLE

The following section describes general considerations for applying cyber resiliency concepts and framework constructs to system life cycle stages and processes.[31] Considerations include addressing the similarities and differences in security and cyber resiliency terminology and how the application of cyber resiliency goals, objectives, techniques, implementation approaches, and design principles can impact systems at key stages in the life cycle. Figure 3 lists the system life cycle processes and illustrates their application across all stages of the system life cycle. It must be emphasized, however, that cyber resiliency engineering does not assume any specific life cycle or system development

---

[31]The system development life cycle introduced in NIST SP 800-64 was withdrawn on May 31, 2019. The current system life cycle is described in [SP 800-160 v1] and is aligned with [ISO 15288).

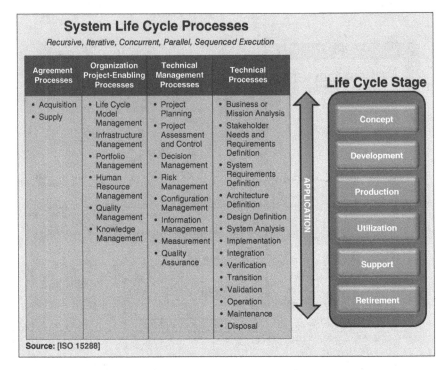

FIGURE 3 System Life Cycle Processes and Life Cycle Stages

process, and cyber resiliency analysis can be performed at any point in and iteratively throughout the life cycle.[32]

Cyber resiliency constructs are interpreted and cyber resiliency engineering practices are applied in different ways depending on the system life cycle stages. During the Concept stage, cyber resiliency goals and objectives are tailored in terms of the concept of use for the system of interest. Tailoring actions are used to elicit stakeholder priorities for the cyber resiliency goals and objectives. The organization's risk management strategy is used to help determine which strategic design principles are most relevant. The strategic design principles and corresponding structural design principles are aligned with design principles from other specialty engineering disciplines. Notional or candidate system architectures are analyzed with respect to how well the

---

[32]See Section 3.2.

prioritized cyber resiliency goals and objectives can be achieved and how well the relevant strategic cyber resiliency design principles can be applied. The tailoring of objectives can also be used to identify or define potential metrics or measures of effectiveness for proposed cyber resiliency solutions. Once again, the risk management strategy that constrains risk response or risk treatment (e.g., commitment to specific technologies, requirements for interoperability with or dependence on other systems) is used to help determine which techniques and approaches can or cannot be used in cyber resiliency solutions. In addition, during the Concept stage, cyber resiliency concerns for enabling systems for production, integration, validation, and supply chain management are identified, and strategies for addressing those concerns are defined.

During the Development stage, the relevant structural cyber resiliency design principles (i.e., those principles that can be applied to the selected system architecture and that support the strategic cyber resiliency design principles) are identified and prioritized based on how well the design principles enable the prioritized cyber resiliency objectives to be achieved. The cyber resiliency techniques and approaches indicated by the structural design principles are analyzed with respect to whether and where they can be used in the selected system architecture given the constraints identified earlier. Cyber resiliency solutions are defined and analyzed with respect to potential effectiveness and compatibility with other aspects of trustworthiness.

Analysis of potential effectiveness considers the relative effectiveness of the solution against potential threat events or scenarios [SP 800-30] and the measures of effectiveness for cyber resiliency objectives. Analysis of compatibility with other aspects of trustworthiness considers potential synergies or conflicts associated with technologies, design principles, or practices specific to other specialty engineering disciplines, particularly security, reliability, survivability, and safety. In addition, specific measures for assessing whether or not the prerequisite requirements have been satisfied within the solution space are defined. This may include, for example, a determination of the baseline reliability of the technology components needed to deliver cyber-resilient capabilities within a system element.

In addition, during the Development stage, the implementation of cyber resiliency solutions is analyzed and evaluated. The verification strategy for cyber resiliency solutions at this stage typically includes adversarial testing or demonstration of mission or business function measures of performance in a stressed environment with adversarial activities. The operational processes and procedures for using technical solutions are defined, refined, and validated with respect to the ability to meet mission and business objectives despite the adversity involving systems containing cyber resources. The cyber resiliency perspective calls for testing and other forms of validation or verification that include adversarial threats among (and in combination with) other stresses on the system. During this life cycle stage, resources (e.g., diverse implementations of critical system elements, alternative processing facilities) required to implement specific courses of action are also developed.

During the Production stage, the verification strategy is applied to instances or versions of the system of interest and associated spare parts or components. The verification strategy for the cyber resiliency requirements as applied to such instances and system elements includes adversarial testing or demonstration in a stressed environment. In addition, during the Production stage, cyber resiliency concerns for enabling systems for production, integration, validation, and supply chain management continue to be identified and addressed.

During the Utilization stage, the effectiveness of cyber resiliency solutions in the operational environment is monitored. Effectiveness may decrease due to changes in the operational environment (e.g., new mission or business processes, new stakeholders, increased user population, configuration drift, deployment in new locations, addition or removal of systems or system elements with which the system of interest interacts), the threat environment (e.g., new threat actors, new vulnerabilities in commonly used technologies), or the technical environment (e.g., the introduction of new technologies into other systems with which the system of interest interacts). Cyber resiliency solutions may need to be adapted to address such changes (e.g., defining new courses of action, reconfiguring system elements, changing mission or business processes and procedures). The relative priorities of cyber resiliency objectives may shift based on changes to stakeholders, stakeholder concerns, mission or business processes, or project funding. Finally, changes in the threat or technical environment may make some techniques or approaches less feasible, while changes in the technical or operational environment may make others more viable.

During the Support stage, maintenance and upgrade of the system or system elements can include integration of new cyber resiliency solutions into the system of interest. This stage also provides opportunities to revisit the prioritization and tailoring of cyber resiliency objectives. Upgrades to or modifications of system capabilities can include significant architectural changes that address accumulated changes to the operational, threat, and technical environments. System modifications and upgrades can also introduce additional vulnerabilities, particularly with architectural changes.

During the Retirement stage, system elements or the entire system of interest are removed from operations. The retirement process can affect other systems with which the system of interest interacts and can decrease the cyber resiliency of those systems and of the supported mission or business processes. Retirement strategies can include phased removal of system elements, turnkey removal of all system elements, phased replacement of system elements, and turnkey replacement of the entire system of interest. Cyber resiliency objectives and priorities are identified for the systems, missions, and business functions in the operational environment to inform analysis of the potential or expected effects of different retirement strategies on the ability to achieve those objectives. Like the support stage, the retirement stage can introduce significant vulnerabilities, particularly during disposal and unintended residue remaining from decommissioned assets.[33]

Table 4 illustrates changes in emphasis for the different cyber resiliency constructs, particularly with respect to cyber resiliency objectives (**bolded**).

TABLE 4 Cyber Resiliency in Life Cycle Stages

Life Cycle Stages	Role of Cyber Resiliency Constructs
CONCEPT	Prioritize and tailor objectives.
	Prioritize design principles and align with other disciplines.
	Limit the set of techniques and approaches to use in solutions.
DEVELOPMENT	Apply design principles to analyze and shape architecture and design.
	Use techniques and approaches to define alternative solutions.
	Develop capabilities to achieve the Prevent/Avoid, Continue, Constrain, Reconstitute, and Understand objectives.

(continued)

---

[33]See [SP 800-88].

TABLE 4 Cyber Resiliency in Life Cycle Stages (*Continued*)

Life Cycle Stages	Role of Cyber Resiliency Constructs
PRODUCTION	Implement and evaluate the effectiveness of cyber resiliency solutions.
	Provide resources (or ensure that resources will be provided) to achieve the Prepare objective.
UTILIZATION	Monitor the effectiveness of cyber resiliency solutions using capabilities to achieve Understand and Prepare objectives.
	Reprioritize and tailor objectives as needed, and adapt mission, business, and/or security processes to address environmental changes (Transform objective).
SUPPORT	Revisit the prioritization and tailoring of objectives; use the results of monitoring to identify new or modified requirements.
	Revisit constraints on techniques and approaches.
	Modify or upgrade capabilities consistent with changes as noted (Re- Architect objective).
RETIREMENT	Prioritize and tailor objectives for the environment of operation.
	Ensure that disposal processes enable those objectives to be achieved, modifying or upgrading capabilities of other systems as necessary (Re- Architect objective).

2.3 RISK MANAGEMENT AND CYBER RESILIENCY

Organizations manage the missions, business functions, and operational risks related to dependencies on systems that include cyber resources as part of a larger portfolio of risks,[34] including financial and reputational risks; programmatic or project-related risks associated with developing a system (e.g., cost, schedule, performance); security risks associated with the organization's mission or business activities, information the organization processes or handles, or requirements arising from legislation, regulations, policies, or standards; and cybersecurity risks. A proposed cyber resiliency solution, while intended primarily to reduce mission, business, or operational risk, can also reduce other types of risk (e.g., security risk, reputational risk, supply chain risk, performance risk). However, like any solution to a risk management

---

[34]These risks are typically addressed by organizations as part of an Enterprise Risk Management (ERM) program. See [IR 8286].

problem, it can also increase other types of risk (e.g., financial, cost, or schedule risk). As part of a multidisciplinary systems engineering effort, systems security engineers and risk management professionals are responsible for articulating the potential adverse impacts of alternative solutions, determining whether those impacts fall within the organizational risk tolerance, deciding whether the adoption of a proposed solution is consistent with the organization's risk management strategy, and informing the organization's risk executive of risk trade-offs.[35]

At the organizational level, a cyber resiliency perspective on risk management can lead to the analysis and management of risks associated with programs and initiatives at multiple levels, which involve investment in, transition to, use of, or transition away from different cyber technologies. The environment in which a system of interest is engineered is rarely static. Related programs, initiatives, or other efforts at federal agencies, driven by [EO 14028], can include efforts to transition to a zero trust architecture, reduce software supply chain risks, and transition from IPv4 to IPv6. Such organization-level programs and initiatives can affect the execution of efforts at lower levels (e.g., an acquisition program for a specific system or service, an initiative to redefine a mission or business process to better accommodate telework).

Motivated by the cyber resiliency Adapt goal, an organization's risk management strategy can also consider the following questions:

- How does each step in a transition plan or an investment plan change the attack surface?
- Are new attack vectors enabled by a given step? How will they be mitigated? Will they be removed in a later step?
- Does this step increase fragility, complexity, or instability? If so, how will those risks be managed?
- On what other programs or initiatives does this step depend? If those efforts do not achieve the expected objectives, how will the risks be managed?
- What new or modified operational procedures and processes are assumed? How will they be resourced and staffed?
- What policy or governance changes are assumed? How will they be achieved? What risks would result if they are not achieved?
- How will the cyber resiliency objectives (as interpreted and prioritized by the organization) continue to be achieved in the face of changes resulting from different programs and initiatives?

---

[35]See Section 3.2.1 and Section C.4.

Generalized Cyber Resiliency Constructs

Cyber resiliency goals, objectives, and techniques are generally defined so they can be applied to all types of threats (not solely cyber threats) and all types of systems (not solely systems that include or are enabled by cyber resources). However, the motivation for these definitions and for the selection of objectives and techniques for inclusion in the cyber resiliency engineering framework is the recognition of dependence on systems involving cyber resources in a threat environment that includes the APT. ▨

Cyber Resiliency in the System Life Cycle

NIST is working with the United States Air Force and the Air Force Research Laboratory (AFRL) to explore ways to incorporate the cyber resiliency constructs in this publication into the system development life cycle through the use of automated support tools. The use of such tools can help ensure that cyber resiliency requirements are clearly defined and more easily integrated into the system development life cycle. Automated tools can provide an efficient and effective vehicle for incorporating cyber resiliency capabilities into a variety of systems (e.g., weapons systems, space systems, command and control systems, industrial control systems, enterprise IT systems) using any established life cycle development process or approach (e.g., agile, waterfall, spiral, DevOps). Automation can also support the rapid testing and evaluation of cyber resiliency capabilities in critical systems to reduce the time to operational deployment. ▨

 CHAPTER THREE

Cyber Resiliency in Practice

Applying Cyber Resiliency Concepts, Constructs, Practices

This chapter identifies considerations for determining which cyber resiliency constructs are most relevant to a system of interest and describes a tailorable process for applying cyber resiliency concepts, constructs, and practices to a system. It also includes guidance on the cyber resiliency analysis carried out during the system life cycle to determine whether the cyber resiliency properties and behaviors of a system of interest, regardless of its life cycle stage, are sufficient for the organization using that system to meet its mission assurance, business continuity, or other security requirements in a threat environment and contested cyberspace that includes the APT.

3.1 SELECTING AND PRIORITIZING CYBER RESILIENCY CONSTRUCTS

The variety of concerns, technologies, and practices related to cyber resiliency results in an extensive framework for cyber resiliency engineering. For example, the engineering framework identifies 14 cyber resiliency techniques and 50 cyber resiliency implementation approaches.

The engineering framework is also complex, with relationships among the constructs of goals, objectives, design principles, techniques, and approaches, as discussed in Appendix D. Cyber resiliency design principles, techniques, and approaches build on, complement, or function in synergy with mechanisms intended to ensure other quality properties (e.g., security, safety, and system resilience).

The variety of circumstances and types of systems for which cyber resiliency can be applied means that no single cyber resiliency technique, approach, or set of approaches is universally optimal or applicable. Systems security engineering seeks to manage risk rather than provide a universal solution. The choice of a risk-appropriate set of cyber resiliency techniques and approaches depends on various trade space considerations and risk factors that are assessed during the systems engineering processes. Employment of all cyber resiliency techniques and approaches is not needed to achieve the cyber resiliency objectives prioritized by stakeholders. In fact, it is not possible to employ all techniques and approaches simultaneously. The following subsections describe factors to consider when selecting a set of cyber resiliency techniques and implementation approaches that best fits the system of interest.

3.1.1 Achievement of Goals and Objectives

Cyber resiliency techniques and associated implementation approaches are employed to achieve mission or business objectives. The relative priorities of cyber resiliency goals and objectives are determined by the mission or business objectives. The selection of specific cyber resiliency techniques and approaches is, therefore, driven in part by the relative priorities of the objectives they support.[36]

3.1.2 Cyber Risk Management Strategy

An organization's cyber risk management strategy (i.e., its strategy for managing risks stemming from dependencies on systems that include cyber resources) is part of its risk management strategy and includes its risk framing for cyber risks.[37] The organization's risk frame identifies which risks or risk factors (i.e., potential impacts or consequences) are unacceptable. For cyber resiliency, the risk frame assumes an adversary with a persistent presence in organizational systems. The risk response portion of the risk management strategy can include priorities or preferences for the types of effects on adversary activities[38] to seek in cyber resiliency solutions.

An organization's risk management strategy is constrained by such factors as legal, regulatory, and contractual requirements as reflected in organizational policies and procedures, financial resources, legacy investments, and organizational culture. These constraints imply the need to consider the costs, ease of use, and operational impacts of security and cyber resiliency solutions. The constraints can be reflected in the selection and tailoring of cyber resiliency techniques, approaches, and design principles. For example, organizational policies and culture can influence whether and how the cyber resiliency technique of Deception is used. The risk management strategy can define an order of precedence for responding to identified risks analogous to the safety order of precedence, such as "harden, sensor, isolate, obfuscate." Together with the strategic design principles selected and specifically tailored to a given program, mission, business function, or system, the order of precedence can guide the selection and application of structural design principles at different locations in an architecture.[39]

---

[36]See Appendix D, Table D-13.
[37]Risk management consists of four major components: risk framing, risk assessment, risk response, and risk monitoring [SP 800-39]. Security risks are considered throughout an organization's enterprise risk management (ERM) process. This includes identifying the risk context; identifying, analyzing, and prioritizing risks; planning and executing risk response strategies; and monitoring, evaluating, and adjusting risk [IR 8286]. Risk response is also referred to as risk treatment [SP 800-160 v1] [ISO 73]. Organizational risk tolerance is determined as part of the risk framing component and defined in the risk management strategy [SP 800-39].
[38]See Appendix F.
[39]See Appendix D.

3.1.3 System Type

The set of cyber resiliency techniques and approaches that are most relevant to and useful in a system depends on the type of system. The following present some general examples of system types and the techniques and approaches that might be appropriate for those types of systems. In addition to the techniques and approaches listed in the examples below, there may be other techniques and approaches that could be useful for a particular type of system. The specific aspects of the system in question will impact the selection as well.

- **Enterprise IT Systems, Shared Services, and Common Infrastructures**

  Enterprise IT (EIT) systems are typically general-purpose computing systems—very often with significant processing, storage, and bandwidth—capable of delivering information resources that can meet the business or other mission needs of an enterprise or a large stakeholder community. As such, all of the cyber resiliency techniques and associated approaches may potentially be viable, although their selection would depend on the other considerations noted in this section.

- **Large-Scale Processing Environments**

  Large-scale processing environments (LSPEs) handle large numbers of events and data (e.g., process transactions) with high confidence in service delivery. The scale of such systems makes them highly sensitive to disruptions to or degradation of service. Therefore, the selective use of the Offloading and Restriction implementations approaches can make the scale of such systems more manageable. This, in turn, will support the application of Analytic Monitoring and the Mission Dependency and Status Visualization approach to Contextual Awareness in a manner that does not significantly affect performance. LSPEs often implement Dynamic Positioning functionality that can be repurposed to help improve cyber resiliency via the Functional Relocation of Cyber Resources, Fragmentation, and Distributed Functionality approaches.

- **System-of-Systems**

  Many cyber resiliency techniques are likely to be applicable to a system-of-systems, but some techniques and approaches can offer greater benefits than others. For example, Contextual Awareness implemented via Mission Dependency and Status Visualization can be applied to predict the potential mission impacts of cyber effects of adversary activities on constituent systems or system elements. The Calibrated

Defense-in-Depth and Consistency Analysis approaches to the technique of Coordinated Protection can help ensure that the disparate protections of the constituent systems operate consistently and in a coordinated manner to prevent or delay the advance of an adversary across those systems. For a system- of-systems involving constituent systems that were not designed to work together and that were developed with different missions, functions, and risk frames, Realignment could also be beneficial. In particular, the Offloading and Restriction approaches could be used to ensure that the core system elements are appropriately aligned to the overall system-of- system mission.

▨ **Critical Infrastructure Systems**

Critical infrastructure systems are often specialized, high confidence, dedicated, purpose- built systems that have highly deterministic properties. Therefore, the availability and integrity of the functionality of the systems are very important as the corruption or lack of availability of some of the key system elements could result in significant harm. For these reasons, techniques adapted from system resilience, such as Redundancy (particularly the Protected Backup and Restore and Surplus Capacity approaches) coupled with aspects of Diversity (e.g., Architectural Diversity, Supply Chain Diversity), could prevent attacks from having mission or business consequences and also maximize the chance of continuation of the critical or essential mission or business operations. Segmentation can isolate highly critical system elements to protect them from an adversary's activities. Approaches such as Trust-Based Privilege Management and Attribute-Based Usage Restriction could constrain the potential damage that an adversary could inflict on a system.

▨ **Cyber-Physical Systems**

As with critical infrastructure systems, cyber-physical systems (CPS) may have limitations regarding storage capacity, processing capabilities, and bandwidth. In addition, many of these systems have a high degree of autonomy with limited human interaction. Some cyber- physical systems operate with no active network connection, although they may connect to a network under specific circumstances (e.g., scheduled maintenance). Non-Persistent Services support the periodic refreshing of software and firmware from a trusted source (e.g., an offline redundant component), in effect flushing out any malware. However, that approach applies only if the organization can allow for the periodic downtime that the refresh would entail. Similarly, the Integrity Checks approach to Substantiated Integrity implemented via cryptographic checksums on critical software could help enable embedded systems to detect corrupted software components.

▪ **Internet of Things**

An Internet of Things (IoT) system consists of system elements with network connectivity and that communicate with an Internet-accessible software application. That software application, which is part of the IoT system, orchestrates the behavior of or aggregates the data provided by constituent system elements. The system elements have limitations in the areas of power consumption, processing, storage capacity, and bandwidth, which in turn may limit the potential for such processing-intensive cyber resiliency approaches such as Obfuscation or Adaptive Management at the device level. Because many "things" (e.g., light bulbs, door locks) are small and relatively simple, they often lack the capacity for basic protection. However, the Integrity Checks approach to Substantiated Integrity could still be viable when applied in conjunction with reliability mechanisms. An IoT system assumes Internet connectivity, although the set of "things" is usually capable of functioning independently if not connected. Because many IoT systems do not assume technical expertise on the part of users, cyber resiliency techniques and approaches that involve human interaction (e.g., Disinformation, Misdirection) may not be appropriate. In addition, the design of IoT systems accommodates flexibility and repurposing of the capabilities of constituent "things." Thus, an application that orchestrated the behavior of one set of "things" may be upgraded to orchestrate additional sets, the members of which were not designed with that application in mind. Such changes to the IoT systems to which that application or the additional sets originally belong can benefit from the application of Realignment. At the level of an IoT system (rather than at the level of individual system elements), Segmentation and Consistency Analysis can be applied.

3.1.4 Cyber Resiliency Conflicts and Synergies

Cyber resiliency techniques can interact in several ways. One technique can depend on another so that the first cannot be implemented without the second; for example, Adaptive Response depends on Analytic Monitoring or Contextual Awareness since a response requires a stimulus. One technique can support another, making the second more effective; for example, Diversity and Redundancy are mutually supportive. One technique can use another so that more design options are available than if the techniques were applied independently; for example, Analytic Monitoring can use Diversity in a design, which includes a diverse set of monitoring tools.

However, one technique can also conflict with or complicate the use of another. For example, Diversity and Segmentation can each make Analytic Monitoring and Contextual Awareness more difficult. A design that incorporates Diversity requires monitoring tools that can handle the diverse set of system elements, while implementation of Segmentation can limit the visibility of such tools. By selecting techniques in accordance with the risk management strategy and design principles, synergies and conflicts between various techniques are taken into consideration. The text below offers three illustrative examples of the interplay, focusing on the techniques that increase an adversary's work factor.

As a first example, Dynamic Positioning and Non-Persistence enable operational agility by making it more difficult for an adversary to target critical resources. These techniques support the Continue, Constrain, and Reconstitute objectives and are part of applying the Support agility and architect for adaptability strategic design principle and the Change or disrupt the attack surface structural design principle. At the same time, these techniques (and the associated implementation approaches) also make it more difficult for an organization to maintain situational awareness of its security posture. That is, Dynamic Positioning and Non-Persistence complicate the use of Contextual Awareness and aspects of Analytic Monitoring and, thus, can conflict with the Maintain situational awareness structural design principle.

As a second example, Redundancy and Diversity together are effective at resisting adversary attacks. These techniques enhance the system's ability to achieve the Continue and Reconstitute objectives and apply the Plan and manage diversity and Maintain redundancy structural design principles. However, the implementation of both Redundancy and Diversity will increase the system's attack surface.

As a final example, Deception can lead the adversary to waste effort and reveal tactics, techniques, and procedures (TTP), but it can also complicate the use of aspects of Analytic Monitoring and Contextual Awareness. In general, while Redundancy, Diversity, Deception, Dynamic Positioning, and Unpredictability will likely greatly increase the adversary work factor, they come at a cost to some other cyber resiliency objectives, techniques, and design principles.

No technique or set of techniques is optimal with respect to all decision factors. There are always ramifications for employing any given technique. The determination of the appropriate selection of techniques is a trade decision that systems engineers make considering all relevant factors. A more complete identification of potential interactions (e.g., synergies and conflicts) between cyber resiliency techniques is presented in Table D-3.

3.1.5 Other Disciplines and Existing Investments

Many of the techniques and implementation approaches that support cyber resiliency are well established. Some technologies or processes are drawn from other disciplines (e.g., Continuity of Operations [COOP], cybersecurity) but are used or executed in a different manner to support cyber resiliency. These include Adaptive Response, Analytic Monitoring, Coordinated Protection, Privilege Restriction, Redundancy, and Segmentation. Others are drawn from disciplines that deal with non-adversarial threats (e.g., safety, reliability). These include Contextual Awareness, Diversity, Non-Persistence, Realignment, and Substantiated Integrity. Still others are cyber adaptations of non-cyber concepts drawn from disciplines that deal with adversarial threats (e.g., medicine, military/defense, sports). These include Deception, Dynamic Positioning, and Unpredictability. Legacy investments made by an organization in these other disciplines can influence which cyber resiliency techniques and approaches are most appropriate to pursue.

3.1.5.1 Investments from Cybersecurity, COOP, and Resilience Engineering

Redundancy-supporting approaches—such as backup, surplus capacity, and replication—are well established in COOP programs. From a cyber resiliency perspective, however, these approaches are not sufficient to protect against the APT. A threat actor might choose to target backup servers as optimum locations to implant malware if those servers are not sufficiently protected. In addition, remote backup servers that employ the same architecture as the primary server are vulnerable to malware that has compromised the primary server. However, if an organization has already invested in backup services (in support of COOP or cybersecurity), those services can be enhanced by requiring an adversary to navigate multiple distinct defenses, authentication challenges (Calibrated Defense-in-Depth approach to Coordinated Protection), or some form of Synthetic Diversity to compensate for known attack vectors.

Contextual Awareness and Analytic Monitoring capabilities are often provided by performance management and cybersecurity functions, including cyber situational awareness, anomaly detection, and performance monitoring. However, the off-the-shelf implementations of these functions are generally insufficient to detect threats from advanced adversaries. Enhancing existing investments in both detection and monitoring by integrating data from sensor and monitor readings from disparate sources is a way to take these existing investments and make them an effective cyber resiliency tool. Another way to make existing technology more cyber- resilient is to complement the existing monitoring services with information from threat intelligence sources, enabling these tools to be better tuned to look for known observables (e.g., indicators of adversary TTPs).

Some approaches to Segmentation and Coordinated Protection appear in information security or cybersecurity. Predefined Segmentation, as reflected in boundary demilitarized zones (DMZs), is a well-established construct in cybersecurity. One important distinction of cyber resiliency is that the segmentation is applied throughout the system, not just at the system boundary. In addition, the Dynamic Segmentation and Isolation approach allows for changing the placement and/or activation of the protected segments. For Coordinated Protection, the defense-in-depth approach is often used for security or system resilience. Ensuring that those protections work in a coordinated fashion is one of the distinguishing aspects of cyber resiliency.

3.1.5.2 Investments from Non-Adversarial Disciplines

Some cyber resiliency techniques and approaches come from disciplines such as safety or performance management. Diversity and certain implementations of Substantiated Integrity, such as Byzantine quorum systems[40] or checksums on critical software, can be traced back to the safety discipline.[41] Therefore, systems that have been designed with safety in mind may already have implemented some of these capabilities. However, the safety capabilities were designed with the assumption that they were countering non-adversarial threat events. To make these capabilities useful against the APT, certain changes are needed. From a safety perspective, it may be sufficient to only employ checksums that are polynomial hash-based (e.g., a cyclic redundancy check used to detect accidental changes) on critical software to ensure that the software has not been corrupted over time. However, such checksums are not sufficient when

---

[40]The National Aeronautics and Space Administration (NASA) Space Shuttle Program applied this concept in multiple computers, which would vote on certain maneuvers.

[41]This is an example of *operational redundancy* where specific failure modes are managed as part of the nominal operation of the system. Redundant Array of Independent Disks (RAID) storage systems and "hyper-converged" computing architectures (i.e., those relying on erasure code for distributed data stores) also fall into this category.

dealing with the APT, which is able to corrupt the software and data and then recalculate or even construct the modified data to duplicate the original checksum. Instead, what is needed in those instances are checksums generated by cryptographic-based secure hash functions that are also cryptographically signed so that they fulfill Integrity Checks and Provenance Tracking to a specified cryptographic strength.

Other capabilities such as Non-Persistence and Adaptive Response are very common in cloud and virtualization architectures. Again, these capabilities were not designed or employed to specifically counter the APT but to facilitate the rapid deployment of implementations. From a system design and implementation perspective, it is easier to employ existing virtualization technology and change the criteria of when and why to refresh critical services (e.g., periodically refresh the software and firmware with the goal of flushing out malware) than it is to deploy Non-Persistence in a system that cannot implement the capability.

3.1.5.3 Investments from Adversarial Disciplines

Several of the cyber resiliency techniques and approaches are cyber adaptions of non-cyber methods used in adversary-oriented disciplines (e.g., medicine, military, sports). These include the Deception, Unpredictability, and Dynamic Positioning techniques and the Dynamic Threat Awareness and Evolvability approaches. None of those techniques or approaches are used in non-adversarial disciplines. There is no reason in resilience engineering to attempt to "mislead" a hurricane, nor is there any benefit in safety engineering to include an element of purposeful unpredictability. The value of these constructs in non-cyber environments is well established. Because these adversarial-derived techniques and approaches are not typically found in disciplines such as safety, resilience engineering, or COOP, it is much more challenging to provide them by enhancing existing constructs. Therefore, they may be more challenging to integrate into an existing system.

3.1.6 Architectural Locations

The selection of cyber resiliency techniques or approaches depends, in part, on where (i.e., at what layers, to which components or system elements, at which interfaces between layers or system elements) in the system architecture cyber resiliency solutions can be applied. The set of layers, like the set of system components or system elements, in an architecture depends on the type of system. For example, an embedded system offers a different set of possible locations than an enterprise architecture that includes applications running in a cloud. The set of layers can include an operational (people-and-processes) layer, a support layer (e.g., programmatic, systems engineering, maintenance, and sustainment), and a layer to represent the physical environment.

Different cyber resiliency techniques or approaches lend themselves to implementation at different architectural layers.[42] Some approaches can be implemented at multiple layers in different ways and with varying degrees of maturity. Other approaches are highly specific to a layer; for example, Asset Mobility is implemented in the operations layer or in the physical environment. For some layers, many approaches may be applicable; for others, relatively few approaches may be available. For example, relatively few approaches can be implemented at the hardware layer. These include Dynamic Reconfiguration, Architectural Diversity, Design Diversity, Replication, Predefined Segmentation, and Integrity Checks.

Similarly, some cyber resiliency approaches lend themselves to specific types of components or system elements. For example, Fragmentation applies to information stores. Some approaches assume that a system element or set of system elements has been included in the architecture specifically to support cyber defense. These include Dynamic Threat Awareness, Forensic and Behavioral Analysis, and Misdirection. Other cyber resiliency approaches assume that a system element has been included in the architecture, explicitly or virtually, to support the mission, security, or business operations. These include Sensor Fusion and Analysis, Consistency Analysis, Orchestration, and all of the approaches to Privilege Restriction.

Finally, some techniques or approaches lend themselves to implementation at interfaces between layers or between system elements. These include Segmentation, Monitoring and Damage Assessment, and Behavior Validation.

3.1.7 Effects on Adversaries, Threats, and Risks

The selection of cyber resiliency techniques and approaches can be motivated by potential effects on adversary activities or on risk. Two resiliency techniques or approaches listed as both potentially having the same effect may differ in how strongly that effect applies to a given threat event, scope (i.e., the set of threat events for which the effect is or can be produced), and affected risk factors. For example, all approaches to Non-Persistence can degrade an adversary's ability to maintain a covert presence via the malicious browser extension TTP; closing

---

[42]See Appendix D, Table D-4.

the browser session when it is no longer needed, a use of Non-Persistent Services, degrades the adversary's activity more than other Non-Persistence approaches do. Some techniques or approaches will affect more risk factors (e.g., reduce the likelihood of impact or reduce the level of impact) than others. The security mechanisms or processes used to implement a particular cyber resiliency approach will also vary with respect to their scope and strength. For example, a Misdirection approach to the Deception technique, implemented via a deception net, and the Sensor Fusion and Analysis approach to Analytic Monitoring, implemented via a holistic suite of intrusion detection systems, will both achieve the detect effect. However, the effectiveness and scope of the two vary widely. For this reason, engineering trade-offs among techniques, approaches, and implementations should consider the actual effects to be expected in the context of the system's architecture, design, and operational environment.

In general, systems security engineering decisions seek to provide as complete a set of effects as possible and to maximize those effects with the recognition that this optimization problem will not have a single solution. The rationale for selecting cyber resiliency techniques or approaches that have complete coverage of the potential effects relates to the long-term nature of the threat campaigns. Potentially, engagements with the APT may go on for months, if not years, possibly starting while a system is in development or even earlier in the life cycle. Given the nature of the threat, its attacks will likely evolve over time in response to a defender's actions. Having a selection of techniques and approaches—where each technique and approach supports (to different degrees and in different ways) multiple effects on the adversary, and the union of the techniques and approaches allows for all potential effects on an adversary— provides the systems engineers with the flexibility to evolve and tailor the effects to the adversary's changing actions. This is analogous to team sports where a team will change its game plan in response to player injuries and the changing game plan of the other team. A team with players who can play multiple positions gives it the flexibility to respond to changes by the opposition and to potentially replace injured players.

Different cyber resiliency techniques and approaches can have different effects on threat events and risk. No single technique or approach can create all possible effects on a threat event, and no technique or approach or set of techniques or approaches can eliminate risk. However, by considering the desired effects, systems engineers can select a set of techniques that will collectively achieve those effects.[43]

---

[43]See Appendix F.

3.1.8 Maturity and Potential Adoption

Approaches to applying cyber resiliency techniques vary in maturity and adoption. The decision to use less mature technologies depends on the organization's risk management strategy and its strategy for managing technical risks. Many highly mature and widely adopted technologies and processes that were developed to meet the general needs of performance, dependability, or security can be used or repurposed to address cyber resiliency concerns. These pose little, if any, technical risk. Changes in operational processes, procedures, and configuration changes may be needed to make these technologies and processes effective against the APT and, thus, part of cyber resiliency solutions.

A growing number of technologies are specifically oriented toward cyber resiliency, including moving target defenses and deception toolkits. These technologies are currently focused on enterprise IT environments. As these technologies become more widely adopted, the decision to include the technologies is influenced more by policy than by technical risk considerations. This is particularly the case for applications of the Deception and Unpredictability cyber resiliency techniques.

Cyber resiliency is an active research area. Technologies are being explored to improve the cyber resiliency of cyber-physical systems, high-confidence, dedicated-purpose systems, and large-scale processing environments. The integration of solutions involving new technologies to reduce risks due to the APT should be balanced against risks associated with perturbing such systems.

 3.2 ANALYTIC PRACTICES AND PROCESSES

In the context of systems security engineering, cyber resiliency analysis is intended to determine whether the cyber resiliency properties and behaviors of a system of interest, regardless of its system life cycle stage, are sufficient for the organization using that system to meet its mission assurance, business continuity, or other security requirements in a threat environment that includes the APT. Cyber resiliency analysis is performed with the expectation that such analysis will support systems engineering and risk management decisions about the system of interest. Depending on the life cycle stage, programmatic considerations, and other factors discussed above, a cyber resiliency analysis could recommend architectural changes, the integration of new products or technologies into the system, changes in how existing products or technologies are used, or changes in operating procedures or environmental protections consistent with and designed to implement the organization's risk management strategy.

The following subsections describe a general, tailorable process for cyber resiliency analysis consisting of steps and tasks, as summarized in Table 5. A variety of motivations for a cyber resiliency analysis are possible, including ensuring that cyber risks due to the APT are fully considered as part of the RMF process or other risk management process, supporting systems security engineering tasks, and recalibrating assessments of risk and risk responses based on information about new threats (e.g., information about a cyber incident or an APT actor), newly discovered vulnerabilities (e.g., discovery of a common design flaw), and problematic dependencies (e.g., discovery of a supply chain issue). Although described in terms of a broad analytic scope, the process can be tailored to have a narrow scope, such as analyzing the potential cyber resiliency improvement that could be achieved by integrating a specific technology or identifying ways to ensure adequate cyber resiliency against a specific threat scenario.

TABLE 5   Tailorable Process for Cyber Resiliency Analysis

Analysis Step	Motivating Question	Tasks
Understand the context	How do stakeholder concerns and priorities translate into cyber resiliency constructs and priorities?	■ Identify the programmatic context. ■ Identify the architectural context. ■ Identify the operational context. ■ Identify the threat context. ■ Interpret and prioritize cyber resiliency constructs.
Establish the initial cyber resiliency baseline	How well is the system doing (i.e., how well does it meet stakeholder needs and address stakeholder concerns) with respect to the aspects of cyber resiliency that matter to stakeholders?	■ Identify existing capabilities. ■ Identify gaps and issues. ■ Define evaluation criteria and make an initial assessment.
Analyze the system	How do cyber risks affect mission, business, or operational risks?	■ Identify critical resources, sources of fragility, and attack surfaces. ■ Represent the adversary perspective.

(continued)

TABLE 5   Tailorable Process for Cyber Resiliency Analysis (*Continued*)

Analysis Step	Motivating Question	Tasks
		▪ Identify and prioritize opportunities for improvement.
Define and analyze specific alternatives	How can mission or operational resilience be improved by improving cyber resiliency?	▪ Define potential technical and procedural solutions. ▪ Define potential solutions for supporting systems and processes. ▪ Analyze potential solutions with respect to criteria.
Develop recommendations	What is the recommended plan of action?	▪ Identify and analyze alternatives. ▪ Assess alternatives. ▪ Recommend a plan of action.

The analytic processes and practices related to cyber resiliency are intended to be integrated with those for other specialty engineering disciplines, including security, systems engineering, resilience engineering, safety, cybersecurity, and mission assurance.[44] In addition, analytic processes and practices related to cyber resiliency can leverage system representations offered by model-based systems engineering (MBSE) and analytic methods (including those involving artificial intelligence [AI] and machine learning [ML]) integrated into MBSE. Cyber resiliency analysis, like other types of engineering analysis (e.g., safety, security), should be performed repeatedly throughout the life cycle as changes arise in the operational, technical, and threat environments.

A variety of artifacts can provide information used in a cyber resiliency analysis depending on its scope, the life cycle stage of the system or systems within the scope of the analysis, the step in the RMF of the in-scope system or systems, the extent to which the organization relying on the system or systems has done contingency planning, and (for systems in the Utilization life cycle stage) reports on security posture and incident response. These artifacts can include engineering project plans, system security plans, supply

---

[44]See Section D.3.

chain risk management plans [SP 800-161], reports on security posture [SP 800-37], penetration test results, contingency plans [SP 800-34], risk analyses [SP 800-30], after-action reports from exercises, incident reports, and recovery plans.

Cyber resiliency analysis complements both system life cycle and RMF tasks. The life cycle and RMF tasks produce information that can be used in cyber resiliency analysis, and cyber resiliency analysis enables cyber risks to be considered more fully in life cycle and RMF tasks.

3.2.1 Understand the Context

The problem of providing sufficient cyber resiliency properties and behaviors is inherently situated in a programmatic, operational, architectural, and threat context. This step is intended to ensure that the context is sufficiently understood and that cyber resiliency constructs can be interpreted in that context, the relative priorities of cyber resiliency objectives can be assessed, and the applicability of cyber resiliency design principles, techniques, and approaches can be determined. The activities in this step can and should be integrated into activities under the Technical Management Processes in [SP 800-160 v1] and the Prepare and Categorize steps of the RMF [SP 800-37].

3.2.1.1 Identify the Programmatic Context

The programmatic context identifies how the system of interest is being acquired, developed, modified, or repurposed, including the life cycle stage, life cycle model, or system development approach (e.g., spiral, waterfall, agile, DevOps). Identification of the life cycle stage, life cycle model, and system development approach enables maturity as a consideration in defining cyber resiliency solutions. The programmatic context also identifies the stakeholders for the system of interest, roles and responsibilities related to the system of interest, and entities (organizations, organizational units, or individuals) in those roles.

In particular, the programmatic context identifies the entities responsible for directing, executing, and determining the acceptability of the results of engineering efforts related to the system (e.g., program office, systems engineer, systems integrator, authorizing official, and mission or business function owner). Each of these key stakeholders has a risk management strategy focused on different potential risks (e.g., cost, schedule, and technical or performance risks for a program office or systems engineer; security risks for an authorizing official; mission or business risks for a mission or business function owner). When these entities are part of the same organization, the risk management strategies for their respective areas of responsibility instantiate or are aligned with the organization's cyber risk management strategy.[45]

Technical or performance risks can include risks that quality properties (e.g., security, safety, system resilience, cyber resiliency) are insufficiently provided, as evidenced by the absence or poor execution of behaviors that should demonstrate those properties. The programmatic risk management strategy can reflect the relative priorities that other stakeholders—in particular, the mission or business process owner and the authorizing official—assign to different quality properties. The programmatic risk management strategy can also include constraints on less mature technologies, less commonly used products, or less commonly applied operational practices as part of managing technical or performance risks.[46]

In addition, other stakeholders may have their own risk management strategies or may be represented by an official within these entities (e.g., a system security officer to represent the security concerns of program managers whose proprietary information is handled by the system of interest) with a corresponding risk management strategy. An appreciation of the different risk management strategies (i.e., how the various stakeholders frame risk, including what threats and potential harms or adverse consequences are of concern to them, what their risk tolerances are, and what risk trade-offs they are willing to make) will enable the threat model to be defined and cyber resiliency constructs to be interpreted and prioritized in subsequent steps.

The programmatic context is not static. Technical, schedule, or security risks can include risks related to other programs or initiatives within the organization, its partners, or its suppliers. The design of the system of interest could assume successful completion of milestones by other programs or initiatives prior to a step in its development, contributing to technical or schedule risks. Schedule slips or failures to meet specific requirements by other programs or initiatives could also increase the attack surface of the system of interest or make it more fragile. Thus, understanding which other programs or initiatives could affect the system of interest is part of identifying the programmatic context.[47]

Identification of the programmatic context highlights the aspects of the programmatic risk management strategy that constrain possible solutions. One aspect is the relative priority of such quality attributes as safety, security,

---

[45]See Section 3.1.2.
[46]See Section 3.1.8.
[47]See Section 2.3.

reliability, maintainability, system resilience, and cyber resiliency. Another is the relative preference for operational changes versus technical changes. Depending on the life cycle stage and the programmatic risk management strategy, changes to operational processes and procedures may be preferred to technical changes to the system.

3.2.1.2 Identify the Architectural Context

The architectural context identifies the type of system; its architecture or architectural patterns, if already defined; and its interfaces with or dependencies on other systems with consideration of whether it is (or is intended to be) part of a larger system-of-systems or a participant in a larger ecosystem. Key technologies, technical standards, or products included (or expected to be included) in the system are identified. Depending on the life cycle stage, identification of the architectural context can also include system locations, sub-systems or components, or layers in the architecture where cyber resiliency solutions could be applied. If this information is not yet available, it will be developed in a subsequent step.[48]

The identification of the type of system begins with the identification of its general type (e.g., CPS,[49] application, enterprise service, common infrastructure as part of EIT or LSPE, EIT as a whole, or LSPE as a whole). The type of system determines which cyber resiliency techniques and approaches are most relevant.[50] Each type of system has an associated set of architectural patterns. For example, a CPS device typically includes a sensor, a controller (which is present in cyberspace), an actuator, and a physical layer. EIT typically includes enterprise services (e.g., identity and access management, mirroring and backup, email), common infrastructures (e.g., an internal communications network, a storage area network, a virtualization, or a cloud infrastructure), a demilitarized zone (DMZ) for interfacing with the Internet, and a collection of enterprise applications.

Identification of other systems with which the system of interest interfaces or on which it depends includes consideration of federation, networking, and scope. Federation typically restricts the set of solutions that can be applied and the metrics that can be defined and used since different system owners may

---

[48]See Section 3.2.3.3.
[49]Multiple levels of aggregation have been defined for CPS: a device, a system, or a system-of-systems [SP 1500-201]. For example, a smart meter is an example of a CPS device; a vehicle is an example of a CPS; and the Smart Grid is an example of a system-of-systems CPS.
[50]See Section 3.1.3.

be unwilling or unable to use the same technologies or share certain types or forms of information. Some systems are designed to operate without a network connection, at least transiently and often normally. The cyber resiliency solutions and means of assessing system cyber resiliency or solution effectiveness will be limited by whether the system is operating in detached mode. Depending on the programmatic context, the scope of "other systems" can include those constituting the system's development, test, or maintenance environment.

3.2.1.3 Identify the Operational Context

The operational context identifies how the system of interest is used or will be used (i.e., its usage context, which is closely related to the architectural context), how it will be administered and maintained (i.e., its support context, which is closely related to the programmatic and architectural contexts), how it interacts with or depends on other systems (i.e., its dependency context), and how usage and dependencies change depending on the time or circumstances (i.e., its temporal context).

The *usage context* identifies the primary mission or business functions that the system supports, any secondary or supporting missions or business functions, and the criticality and reliability with which the missions or business functions are to be achieved. Thus, the usage context can:

▨ Describe the system in terms of its intended uses, which include not only its primary mission or business function but also secondary or likely additional uses. The description includes the identification of external interfaces—to networks, other supporting infrastructures and services, and end users—in a functional sense, keeping in mind that these interfaces can vary.

▨ Describe the system's criticality to its missions, stakeholders, end users, or the general public. Criticality is "an attribute assigned to an asset that reflects its relative importance or necessity in achieving or contributing to the achievement of stated goals" [SP 800-160 v1] and relates strongly to the potential impacts of system malfunction, degraded or denied performance, or not performing to the missions it supports, human life or safety, national security, or economic security (e.g., as in the context of critical infrastructure [NIST CSF]).

▨ Identify whether the system is or contains a high-value asset (HVA) (e.g., as defined in [OMB M-19-03], repositories of large volumes of PII or financial assets) or plays a central role (even if non-critical) in a critical infrastructure sector (e.g., financial services, Defense Industrial Base [DIB]) since these characteristics could attract specific types of adversaries.

▪ If possible, identify measures of effectiveness (MOEs) and measures of performance (MOPs) for organizational missions or business functions. Cyber resiliency effectiveness metrics, which can be defined and used later in the analysis process,[51] can sometimes repurpose mission MOEs, MOPs, or data collected to evaluate MOEs and MOPs and can often be related to MOEs and MOPs, particularly for cyber resiliency metrics related to Withstand or Recover.

The usage context also provides a general characterization of the system user population, including its size, scope, and assumed user awareness of and ability to respond to cyber threats. The usage context also indicates whether cyber defenders are actively involved in monitoring the system and responding to indications and warnings (I&W) of adverse conditions or behaviors.

The *support context* similarly provides a general characterization of the administrative and maintenance population, describes how system maintenance or updates are performed, and describes operational restrictions on maintenance activities or updates. For example, updates to embedded control units (ECUs) in a vehicle should be disallowed when driving. These aspects of the operational context determine the extent to which procedural solutions can be applied to the system of interest.

The *dependency context* identifies adjacent systems (i.e., systems with which the system of interest is connected, for example, through procedure calls or information sharing); describes the types of information received from, supplied to, or exchanged with those systems; and identifies the criticality of the information connection to the system of interest and to the mission or business functions it supports. The dependency context also identifies infrastructures on which the system of interest depends (e.g., networks, power suppliers, and environmental control systems). These aspects of the operational context are used to bound the scope of the analysis (e.g., whether and for which adjacent or infrastructure systems changes are in scope, whether characteristics and behavior of these systems can be investigated or must be assumed). If the system of interest is part of a system-of-systems or is a participant in a larger ecosystem, the dependency context identifies the implications of aggregation

---

[51]See Section 3.2.2.3 and Section 3.2.4.3.

or federation for governance, system administration, and information sharing with other organizations or systems.

The *temporal context* identifies whether and how the usage and dependency contexts can change, depending on whether the system is operating under normal, stressed, or maintenance conditions; whether the system is being used for one of its secondary purposes; and how the system's usage and dependencies change over time during the course of executing mission or business functions.

Information about the support and dependency contexts can be used at this point in the analysis to characterize and subsequently identify the system's attack surfaces.[52] The operational context can be communicated by defining a motivating operational scenario or a small set of operational scenarios.

3.2.1.4 Identify the Threat Context

The threat context identifies threat sources, threat events, and threat scenarios of concern for the system of interest. In particular, the threat context helps to identify the characteristics and behaviors of adversaries whose attacks would necessarily undermine the system's ability to execute or support its missions, as well as the characteristics of relevant non-adversarial threats. Adversaries can include insiders as well as individuals or groups located outside of the system's physical and logical security perimeter. Adversary goals are identified and translated into cyber and mission effects. Adversary behaviors (i.e., threat events, attack scenarios, or TTPs) are also identified.

The threat context can:

- Identify the types of threats considered in programmatic or organizational risk framing. In addition to adversarial threats, these can include non-adversarial threats of human error, faults and failures, and natural disasters. A cyber resiliency analysis can identify scenarios in which adversaries can take advantage of the consequences of non-adversarial threat events.
- Identify the adversary's characteristics, to construct an adversary profile. Characteristics can include the adversary's ultimate goals and intended cyber effects, the specific time frame over which the adversary operates, the adversary's persistence (or, alternately, how easily the adversary can be deterred, discouraged, or redirected to a different target), the adversary's concern for stealth, and the adversary's targeting, which relates to

---

[52]See Section 3.2.3.1.

the scope or scale of the effects that the adversary intends to achieve. Note that multiple adversaries can be profiled.

▪ Identify the types of threat events or adversarial behaviors of concern. Behaviors are described in terms of adversary TTPs and can be categorized using the categories of the Adversarial Tactics, Techniques, and Common Knowledge (ATT&CK™) framework [Strom17] or .govCAR [DHSCDM].

▪ Identify the potential attack scenarios of concern and describe each scenario with a phrase or a sentence. A set of attack scenarios (e.g., as identified in [Bodeau18a] [Bodeau16]) can serve as a starting point. The attack scenarios of concern in the cyber resiliency use case should be clearly related to the system's mission. Note that a cyber resiliency analysis can focus on a single attack scenario or consider a set of scenarios.

A threat model can also include potential threat scenarios related to non-adversarial threat sources. For these threat sources, the scope or scale of effects, duration or time frame, and types of assets affected are identified. If possible, provide a reference to a publicly available description of a similar scenario to serve as an anchoring example.

Depending on its scope and purpose, a cyber resiliency analysis can focus on a single threat scenario. For example, a cyber resiliency analysis can be motivated by a publicized incident with the purpose of the analysis being to determine the extent to which a particular system, mission or business function, or organization could be affected by a similar incident.

3.2.1.5 Interpret and Prioritize Cyber Resiliency Constructs

To ensure that cyber resiliency concepts and constructs are meaningful in the identified contexts, one or more of the following sub-tasks can be performed:

▪ Restate and prioritize cyber resiliency objectives[53] and sub-objectives.[54] Identify, restate, and prioritize capabilities or activities that are needed to achieve relevant sub-objectives based on the identified threat context. These constructs are restated in terms that are meaningful in the architectural and operational contexts and prioritized based on programmatic considerations and stakeholder concerns. Note that responsibility for some capabilities or activities may be allocated to system elements outside of the

---

[53]See Section 3.1.1.
[54]See Appendix D, Table D-1.

scope of the engineering or risk management decisions that the cyber resiliency analysis is intended to support.

▦ Determine the potential applicability of cyber resiliency design principles. This involves considering organizational and programmatic risk management strategies to determine which strategic design principles may apply. It also involves considering the architecture, operational context, and threat environment to identify the relevance of structural design principles to this situation. Relevant structural design principles are restated in situation- specific terms (e.g., in terms of the technologies that are part of the system).

▦ Determine the potential applicability of cyber resiliency techniques and (depending on the level of detail with which the architectural context is defined) implementation approaches. This involves considering the architecture, operational context, and threat context. The relevance of the techniques and of the approaches to this situation is described and assessed. Relevant techniques and approaches can be restated and described in terms of architectural elements (e.g., allocating an implementation approach to a specific system element or identifying an architectural layer at which a technique can be applied). However, detailed descriptions are generally deferred to a later stage in a cyber resiliency analysis.[55]

The determination that some cyber resiliency constructs are not applicable, based on the considerations discussed in Section 3.1, narrows the focus of subsequent steps in the cyber resiliency analysis, which saves work and increases the usefulness of the results.

3.2.2 Develop the Cyber Resiliency Baseline

In order to determine whether cyber resiliency improvement is needed, the baseline for the system (as it is understood at the stage in the life cycle when the cyber resiliency analysis is performed) must be established.

3.2.2.1 Establish the Initial Cyber Resiliency Baseline

As discussed in Section 3.1.5.1, a system reflects architectural and design decisions and investments in specific technologies and products motivated by other specialty engineering disciplines. Capabilities are identified from such

---

[55]See Section 3.2.3.3.

functional areas as COOP and contingency planning; security, cybersecurity, and cyber defense; performance management; reliability, maintainability, and availability (RMA); safety; and survivability. Identification of capabilities can involve decomposition of the system of interest into constituent sub-systems, functional areas, and/or architectural locations.[56]

Capabilities can be characterized in terms of the cyber resiliency techniques and approaches they can implement and/or the cyber resiliency design principles they can be used to apply. Capabilities can also be characterized in terms of how easily their configuration or operational use can be adapted to address specific cyber resiliency concerns, how dynamically they can be reconfigured or repurposed, and how compatible they are with other cyber resiliency techniques and approaches (e.g., deception, unpredictability).

3.2.2.2 Identify Gaps and Issues

Depending on the life cycle stage, issues may already be tracked, or it may be possible to identify gaps in required capabilities and issues with the system's design, implementation, or use. Such information can be found in after-action reports from exercises, penetration test reports, incident reports, and reporting related to ongoing assessments and ongoing risk response actions (RMF tasks M-2 and M-3) [SP 800-37]. Security gaps may also have been identified from a coverage analysis with respect to a taxonomy of attack events or TTPs [DHSCDM].

Because senior leadership is often aware of issues and gaps, recommended cyber resiliency solutions will need to be characterized in terms of how and how well the solutions address the issues and gaps, as well as in terms of other benefits that the recommended solutions provide (e.g., improved stability, improved performance).

3.2.2.3 Define Evaluation Criteria and Make Initial Assessment

One or more evaluation criteria are established and used to make an initial assessment. Cyber resiliency can be evaluated in multiple ways, including:

- How well the system achieves (or, assuming it meets its requirements, will achieve) cyber resiliency objectives and sub-objectives (considering the priority weighting established earlier).[57] An initial assessment can be expressed as high-level qualitative assessments (e.g., on a scale from Very

---

[56]See Section 3.1.6.
[57]See Section 3.2.1.5.

Low to Very High) for the cyber resiliency objectives and subsequently refined based on analysis of the system. An initial assessment can also take the form of a cyber resiliency coverage map that indicates whether and how well the cyber resiliency constructs that were determined to be relevant have been applied.[58] Alternately (if the information is available) or subsequently (based on the analysis described in Section 3.2.3.1 and Section 3.2.3.3),[59] this assessment can be expressed as a cyber resiliency score.

▪ How well the system's capabilities cover (i.e., have at least one effect on) adversary activities as identified by the threat context.[60] This can be expressed as a threat heat map [DHSCDM] or a simple threat coverage score. For an initial assessment, coverage can be in terms of attack stages.[61] Alternately or subsequently, a more nuanced threat coverage score based on the organization's risk management strategy can be computed using the relative priorities of the general types of effects (e.g., increase adversary cost, decrease adversary benefits, increase adversary risk) and of the specific effects (e.g., redirect, preclude, impede, detect, limit, expose) if the risk management strategy establishes such priorities.

▪ The level of cyber risk in terms of risk to missions, business functions, or other forms of risk (e.g., security, safety, reputation). An assessment of this form is possible if the organization has established a risk model, or at least a consequence model, for such forms of risk. An initial assessment will typically rely on an existing security risk assessment [SP 800-30].

▪ The level of operational resilience (i.e., mission or business function resilience) in terms of functional performance measures under stress. An assessment of this form is possible if the organization has established such performance measures. An initial assessment will typically rely on an existing performance assessment, which describes operational resilience in the face of prior incidents and will be subject to uncertainty since prior incidents may be poor predictors of future ones.

Additional evaluation criteria can consider how well the system meets its security requirements or achieves its security objectives and how well the system satisfies its mission or business function requirements. While such

---

[58]See Section 3.2.1.5.
[59]See Section 3.2.4.3.
[60]See Appendix F.
[61]See Section F.2.

evaluations are independent of cyber resiliency analysis, they can form part of the baseline against which potential solutions can be evaluated.

Stakeholder concerns and priorities are used to determine which (or which combination) of these will be used to evaluate alternative solutions. Approaches to assessment (e.g., scoring systems, qualitative assessment scales, metrics and measures of effectiveness) and candidate metrics can be identified for use in subsequent steps. In addition, evaluation criteria can involve assessments of potential costs in terms of financial investment over subsequent life cycle stages (e.g., acquiring, integrating, operating, and maintaining a cyber resiliency solution), opportunity costs (e.g., constraints on future engineering decisions or system uses), and increased programmatic risk (e.g., potential cost risk, schedule impacts, performance impacts).

3.2.3 Analyze the System

In this step, the system is analyzed in its operational context from two perspectives. First, a mission or business function perspective is applied to identify critical resources (i.e., those resources for which damage or destruction would severely impact operations) and sources of system fragility. Second, an adversarial perspective is applied to identify high-value primary and secondary targets of APT actors [OMB M-19-03] and develop representative attack scenarios.

Based on this analysis and the results of the previous baseline assessment, opportunities for improvement are identified.

3.2.3.1 Identify Critical Resources, Sources of Fragility, and Attack Surfaces

A critical resource can be a resource for which damage (e.g., corruption or reduced availability), denial of service, or destruction results in the inability to complete a critical task. In addition, if a resource is used in multiple tasks, it can be highly critical overall even if it is not critical to any of those functions individually if its damage, denial, or destruction results in a delay for a time-critical mission or business function. Critical resources can be identified using a variety of methods specific to contingency planning, resilience engineering, and mission assurance. These include Criticality Analysis [IR 8179], Mission Impact Analysis (MIA), Business Impact Analysis (BIA) [SP 800-34], Crown Jewels Analysis (CJA), and cyber mission impact analysis (CMIA).

For cyber resiliency analysis, the identification of critical resources is based on an understanding of functional flows or of mission or business function threads. A resource can be highly critical at one point in a functional flow or a mission thread and of very low criticality at other points. A functional flow analysis or a mission thread analysis can reveal such time dependencies.

Systems can also be analyzed to identify sources of fragility or brittleness. While identification of single points of failure is a result of the analysis methods mentioned above, network analysis or graph analysis (i.e., analysis of which system elements are connected, how and how tightly the system elements are connected, and whether some sets of system elements are more central) can determine whether the system is fragile (i.e., whether it will break if a stress beyond a well- defined set is applied). Similarly, graphical analysis of the distribution of different types of components can help determine how easily a given stress (e.g., exploitation of a zero-day vulnerability) could propagate.

Finally, the attack surfaces to which cyber resiliency solutions can be applied can be identified. Information about the programmatic, architectural, and operational context determines which attack surfaces are within the scope of potential cyber resiliency solutions. For example, if the programmatic context determines support systems to be in scope, those systems are an attack surface in addition to the interfaces and procedures by which updates are made to the system of interest; if the system of interest is an enterprise service (architectural context), its interfaces to other services on which it depends as well as to applications which use it are also attack surfaces; if the system has users (operational context), the user community is an attack surface.[62]

3.2.3.2 Represent the Adversary Perspective

Cyber resiliency analysis assumes an architectural, operational, and threat context for the system being analyzed.[63] These contextual assumptions provide the starting point for a detailed analysis of how an adversary could affect the system and thereby cause harm to the mission or business functions it supports, the organization, individuals for whom the system handles PII or whose safety depends on the system, or the operational environment. The attack scenarios of concern that were identified as part of the threat context serve as a starting point.[64] Depending on the scope of the analysis,[65] these attack scenarios can be complemented by scenarios driven by adversary goals, scenarios targeting critical assets or high-value assets,[66] or scenarios that take advantage of sources of fragility.

---

[62]See Section D.5.1.3.
[63]See Section 3.2.1.
[64]See Section 3.2.1.4.
[65]As noted in Section 3.2.1.4, a cyber resiliency analysis can be focused on a single attack scenario.
[66]See OMB M-19-03.

The adversary perspective (i.e., what harm can be done, how easily, and at what cost to the attacker) can be represented in different ways, depending on the stage of the system life cycle and the corresponding level and amount of information about the system architecture, design, implementation, and operations. At a minimum, an attack scenario can identify stages in the attack (e.g., administer, engage, persist, cause effect, and maintain ongoing presence), the adversary objectives or categories of TTPs at each stage (e.g., reconnaissance, exploitation, lateral movement, denial), and the system elements compromised in each stage. Depending on the system life cycle stage, it may be possible to identify individual TTPs (e.g., pass the hash) or examples of specific malware.[67]

Attack scenarios can be represented as part of a model-based engineering effort; using attack tree or attack graph analysis; in terms of fault tree analysis or failure modes, effects, and criticality analysis (FMECA); or based on the identification of loss scenarios from System- Theoretic Process Analysis (STPA). Common elements across the attack scenarios (e.g., recurring adversary TTPs) can be starting points for identifying potential alternative solutions.

Depending on the scope of the cyber resiliency analysis, attack scenarios can be developed that target supporting systems. Such attack scenarios may be the result of a supply chain risk analysis or a cyber resiliency or cybersecurity analysis of systems or organizations responsible for development, integration, testing, or maintenance.

3.2.3.3 Identify and Prioritize Opportunities for Improvement

The identification of potential areas of improvement typically relies on the interpretation and prioritization of cyber resiliency constructs performed earlier.[68] Potential cyber resiliency techniques or implementation approaches can be identified in system-specific terms, mapped to system elements or architectural layers, and stated as desired improvements to system elements or to the system as a whole. Desired improvements are prioritized based on how and how well they are expected to reduce risks as identified by stakeholders.[69]

---

[67]However, specific malware should be treated as a motivating example only. Cyber resiliency engineering assumes that unforeseen malware can be used and seeks to mitigate types of adversary actions.

[68]See Section 3.2.1.5.

[69]See Section 3.2.1.1.

In more detail, this task in the analysis process can include the following sub-tasks:

▥ Identify potentially applicable techniques or approaches. If the set of potentially applicable techniques and approaches has already been identified,[70] it can be narrowed by identifying the set of techniques and approaches related to prioritized objectives using Appendix D, Table D-13 or to potentially applicable structural design principles using Table D-15. (If only the applicable strategic design principles were identified, Table D-14 can be used to identify relevant objectives and Table D-10 can be used to identify relevant structural design principles.) Otherwise, the set of techniques and approaches related to prioritized objectives or structural design principles can be refined by taking the architectural and programmatic context into consideration. The potentially applicable techniques or approaches are described in system-specific terms.

▥ Identify locations where cyber resiliency solutions could be applied.[71] The set of locations (i.e., sub-systems or components, layers in the architecture, or interfaces between sub- systems or between layers) where cyber resiliency solutions could be applied is determined by the system architecture as constrained by context.[72] For example, the programmatic context may prioritize cyber resiliency solutions that change how existing technologies are used over changes to the system architecture (e.g., replacing specific system elements); the architectural context may restrict locations to specific interfaces (e.g., if the system of interest is an enterprise service, solutions may be applied to its interfaces with sub-systems or applications that use it or with supporting services, particularly security services); or the operational context may constrain the extent to which new user procedures can be made part of the system (e.g., depending on the size of, cyber expertise of, or organizational control over the user population).

▥ Identify desired improvements to system elements or to the system of interest as a whole. Statements of desired improvements described in terms specific to the architectural and operational context can be more meaningful to stakeholders than general statements about improved use of a cyber resiliency technique or a more effective application of a cyber resiliency design principle. Potential improvements can be described in

---

[70]See Section 3.2.1.5.
[71]See Section 3.1.6.
[72]See Section 3.2.1.

terms of improved protection for critical resources, reduced fragility, or the ability to address threats more effectively.

▪ Prioritize desired improvements using the identified evaluation criteria (e.g., improve the ability of a given system element to continue functioning by enabling that element to be dynamically isolated, decrease adversary benefits by reducing the concentration of highly sensitive information in a single asset, or reduce mission risks by providing extra resources for high-criticality tasks).

3.2.4 Define and Analyze Specific Alternatives

In this step, specific ways to make desired improvements (i.e., architectural changes, ways to implement cyber resiliency techniques in the context of the existing architecture, ways to use existing system capabilities more effectively to improve resilience) are identified and analyzed in terms of potential effectiveness. These specific alternatives form a solution set that will be used in the final step to construct potential courses of action.

3.2.4.1 Define Potential Technical and Procedural Solutions

Potential applications of cyber resiliency techniques and implementation approaches to the system of interest in its environment of operations in order to provide one or more desired improvements are identified.[73] These applications (i.e., potential solutions to the problem of improving mission or operational resilience by improving cyber resiliency) can be purely technical, purely procedural, or combinations of the two.

Potential solutions can incorporate or build on investments from other disciplines.[74] The set of technologies and products that is available at some level of maturity[75] for incorporation into the system depends on the system type.[76] The degree to which relatively immature technologies can be considered depends on the programmatic risk management strategy.[77]

The level of detail with which a potential solution is described depends on how specifically the context was described in the first step.[78] In particular, if the architectural and operational contexts were described in general terms,

---

[73]See Section 3.2.3.3.
[74]See Section 3.1.5.
[75]See Section 3.1.8.
[76]See Section 3.1.3.
[77]See Section 2.3 and Section 3.2.1.1.
[78]See Section 3.2.1.

potential solutions will necessarily be described at a high level. Alternatively, if the cyber resiliency analysis is being performed for an existing system, a potential solution can be described in terms of specific technologies or products to be integrated into the system, where in the system those technologies will be used, how they will interface with other system elements, configuration settings or ranges of settings for products, and processes or procedures to make effective use of existing or newly acquired technologies.

The description of a potential solution can include identification of the gaps it is expected to address,[79] the threats (e.g., attack scenarios, adversary objectives or categories of TTPs, or adversary actions) it is intended to address,[80] or the reduced exposure of critical resources, sources of fragility, or attack surfaces to threats.[81] These different elements of a potential solution's description can be used to evaluate the solution.[82]

3.2.4.2 Define Potential Solutions for Supporting Systems and Processes

If programmatic and operational contexts support improvements to supporting systems and processes, the potential applications of cyber resiliency techniques and approaches to these systems and processes are also identified. Such applications can include modifications to contracting to help ensure that controlled unclassified information (CUI) or other sensitive information is protected [SP 800-171], improvements to supply chain risk management (SCRM) as determined by SCRM analysis [SP 800-161], and restrictions on or re-architecting of system development, testing, or maintenance environments to improve the cyber resiliency of those environments.

3.2.4.3 Analyze Potential Solutions with Respect to Criteria

Potential solutions can be analyzed with respect to one or more criteria.[83] Evaluation can employ qualitative or semi-quantitative assessments (using subject matter expert [SME] judgments) or quantitative metrics (evaluated in a model-based environment, laboratory, cyber range, or test environment; metrics to support analysis of alternatives are typically not evaluated in an

---

[79]See Section 3.2.2.2.
[80]See Section 3.2.3.2.
[81]See Section 3.2.3.1.
[82]See Section 3.2.4.3.
[83]See Section 3.2.2.3.

operational environment). For example, potential solutions can be analyzed to determine:

▪ How much the solution could improve the ability of the system to achieve its (priority- weighted) cyber resiliency objectives or sub-objectives. This can be expressed as a change in a cyber resiliency score or as a coverage map for the relevant cyber resiliency constructs. Alternately or in support of scoring, performance metrics for activities or capabilities related to cyber resiliency sub-objectives can be evaluated.

▪ How well the system, with the solution applied, addresses adversary activities or attack scenarios as identified by the threat context. As noted in Section 3.2.2.3, this can take the form of a threat heat map or a threat coverage score using a taxonomy of adversary activities (e.g., [MITRE18]). It can also take the form of an adversary return on investment (ROI) score or a more nuanced threat coverage score.[84] Alternately or in support of scoring, performance metrics for specific types of effects on adversary actions can be defined and evaluated before and after the solution is applied (e.g., length of time it takes an adversary to move laterally across a system or an enclave).

▪ How much the solution could improve the system's coverage of adversary TTPs using capabilities defined in [NIST CSF]. This can be expressed as a change in a score or using a threat heat map [DHSCDM].

▪ How much the solution could decrease the level of cyber risk or a specific component of risk (e.g., level of consequence). As discussed in Appendix F,[85] effects on adversary activities have associated effects on risk.

▪ How much the solution could improve the level of operational resilience in terms of functional performance measures under stress. As discussed in Section D.5.1, some strategic design principles for cyber resiliency are closely related to design principles for Resilience Engineering. Thus, a solution that applies one or more of those design principles can be expected to improve resilience against non-adversarial as well as adversarial threats.

▪ Whether and how much the solution could improve the system's ability to meet its security requirements. Evaluation with respect to this criterion can involve qualitative assessments by subject matter experts (SME), an explanatory description, a list of previously unmet requirements that the

---

[84]See Appendix F.
[85]See Table F-1.

solution can help meet, or specific security performance metrics that can be evaluated before and after the solution is applied.

▪ Whether and how much the solution could improve the system's ability to meet its mission or business function performance requirements. Similar to a security requirements criterion, evaluation with respect to this criterion can involve an explanatory description, qualitative assessments by SMEs, a list of previously unmet requirements that the solution can help meet, or specific functional performance metrics that can be evaluated before and after the solution is applied.

In addition, the potential costs of a solution can be identified or assessed. The product of this step is a list of alternative solutions, with each alternative characterized (e.g., using a coverage map or a description) or assessed with respect to the identified criteria.

3.2.5 Develop Recommendations

This step results in a plan of action to address recommended implementation approaches. Unless the scope of the cyber resiliency analysis is narrow, the number and variety of potential solutions may be large. Potential solutions that could be implemented at the same time can be constructed and analyzed to ensure compatibility, identify possible synergies, and determine whether specific solutions should be applied sequentially rather than simultaneously. In addition, programmatic and operational risks associated with alternative solutions can be identified.

3.2.5.1 Identify and Analyze Alternatives

One or more alternatives (i.e., sets of potential solutions that could be implemented at the same time or sequentially such as in successive spirals) can be identified using either total cost or a requirement for a consistent level of maturity[86] (e.g., requiring all technical solutions in the set to be available as commercial products by a specific milestone) to bound each set. Where possible, a set of potential solutions should be defined to take advantage of synergies (as discussed in Section 3.1.4 and identified in Appendix D, Table D-3). At a minimum, each set should be analyzed to ensure that there are no internal

---

[86]See Section 3.1.8.

conflicts. If the solutions in a set are to be implemented sequentially, functional dependencies among those solutions should be identified. In addition, functional dependencies on other system elements (particularly those involving investments due to other disciplines)[87] should be identified since changes in system elements can be made for a variety of reasons. Finally, functional dependencies on other organizational efforts (e.g., programs, initiatives) should be identified to ensure that changes to the attack surfaces of the system of interest, the organization's infrastructure and supporting services, and other systems or assets are understood and the associated risks managed.[88]

3.2.5.2 Assess Alternatives

Each alternative can be assessed or characterized in terms of the evaluation criteria.[89] To support assessments, the adversarial analysis[90] can be revisited for each alternative. Due to synergies or other interactions between cyber resiliency techniques, changes in scores, heat maps, or coverage maps must be determined by analysis rather than by simply combining previously determined values. In addition, each alternative should be analyzed to determine whether it makes new attack scenarios (or non-adversarial threat scenarios) possible. If it does, those scenarios should be analyzed to determine whether changes should be made to the alternative.

Each alternative can also be described in terms of the issues it resolves, the gaps it fills,[91] or whether it provides improved protection for critical resources, reduced fragility, or the ability to address threats more effectively. Finally, each alternative can be assessed or described in terms of its effects on programmatic risk (e.g., total costs, changes to schedule risk, changes to technical or performance risk) or other risks of concern to stakeholders. If an alternative diverges from the risk management strategies of one or more stakeholders, this divergence should be noted so that a compensating risk management approach can be made part of the recommendation if the alternative is in fact recommended.

---

[87]See Section 3.1.5.
[88]See Section 2.3.
[89]See Section 3.2.4.3.
[90]See Section 3.2.3.2.
[91]See Section 3.2.2.2.

3.2.5.3 Recommend a Plan of Action

A recommended plan of action resulting from a cyber resiliency analysis can take the form of a set of selected alternatives to be implemented in successive phases. For each phase, the costs, benefits, and risk management approaches can be identified, accompanied by the identification of circumstances that could indicate the need to revisit the recommendations. However, as noted in Section 3.1, a cyber resiliency analysis can be narrowly focused. If this is the case, the recommendations resulting from the analysis will take a form directed by the focus of the analysis.

 REFERENCES

Laws, Policies, Directives, Regulations, Standards, and Guidelines

Laws and Executive Orders	
[FISMA]	Federal Information Security Modernization Act (P.L. 113-283), December 2014.
	https://www.govinfo.gov/app/details/PLAW-113publ283
[FOIA96]	Freedom of Information Act (FOIA), 5 U.S.C. § 552, As Amended By Public Law No. 104-231, 110 Stat. 3048, Electronic Freedom of Information Act Amendments of 1996.
	https://www.govinfo.gov/app/details/PLAW-104publ231
[EO 13800]	Executive Order 13800 (2017), Strengthening the Cybersecurity of Federal Networks and Critical Infrastructure. (The White House, Washington, DC), DCPD-201700327, May 11, 2017.
	https://www.govinfo.gov/app/details/DCPD-201700327
[EO 14028]	Executive Order 14028 (2021), Improving the Nation's Cybersecurity. (The White House, Washington, DC), May 12, 2021.
	https://www.federalregister.gov/d/2021-10460
Regulations, Directives, Instructions, Plans, and Policies	
[OMB A-130]	Office of Management and Budget (2016) Managing Information as a Strategic Resource (The White House, Washington, DC), OMB Circular A-130, July 2016.
	https://www.whitehouse.gov/sites/whitehouse.gov/files/omb/circulars/A130/a13 0revised.pdf

[CNSSI 1253] Committee on National Security Systems (2014) Security Categorization and Control Selection for National Security Systems. (National Security Agency, Fort George G. Meade, MD), CNSS Instruction 1253. https://www.cnss.gov/CNSS/issuances/Instructions.cfm

[CNSSI 4009] Committee on National Security Systems (2015) Committee on National Security Systems (CNSS) Glossary. (National Security Agency, Fort George G. Meade, MD), CNSS Instruction 4009. https://www.cnss.gov/CNSS/issuances/Instructions.cfm

[HSPD23] National Security Presidential Directive/NSPD-54 Homeland Security Presidential Directive/HSPD-23, Cybersecurity Policy, January 2008.

[OMB M-19-03] Office of Management and Budget (2018) Management of High Value Assets. (The White House, Washington, DC), OMB Memorandum M-19-03, December 2018.

https://www.whitehouse.gov/wp-content/uploads/2018/12/M-19-03.pdf

[PPD8] Presidential Policy Directive (PPD) 8, *National Preparedness*, March 2011, last published August 2018.

https://www.dhs.gov/presidential-policy-directive-8-national-preparedness

[FMRS20] Federal Mission Resilience Strategy 2020, December 2020.

https://www.hsdl.org/?view&did=848323

[PPD21] Presidential Policy Directive (PPD) 21, *Critical Infrastructure Security and Resilience*, February 2013.

https://obamawhitehouse.archives.gov/the-press-office/2013/02/12/presidential- policy-directive-critical-infrastructure-security-and-resil

Standards, Guidelines, and Reports

[IEC 62443-3-3] International Electrotechnical Commission (2013) *IEC 62443-3-3:2013, Industrial communication networks – Network and system security – Part 3-3: System security requirements and security levels.* https://webstore.iec.ch/publication/7033

[IEC 62443-4-2] International Electrotechnical Commission (2019) *IEC 62443-4-2:2019, Security for industrial automation and control systems – Part 4-2: Technical security requirements for IACS components.* https://webstore.iec.ch/publication/34421

[ISO 73] International Organization for Standardization (2009) *ISO Guide 73:2009 – Risk management – Vocabulary* (ISO, Geneva, Switzerland). https://www.iso.org/standard/44651.html

[ISO 15288] International Organization for Standardization/International Electrotechnical Commission/Institute of Electrical and Electronics Engineers (2015) *ISO/IEC/IEEE 15288:2015 – Systems and software engineering — Systems life cycle processes* (ISO, Geneva, Switzerland). https://www.iso.org/standard/63711.html

[ISO 24765]   International Organization for Standardization/International
               Electrotechnical Commission/Institute of Electrical and Electronics
               Engineers (2017) *ISO/IEC/IEEE 24765-2017 – Systems and software
               engineering – Vocabulary* (ISO, Geneva, Switzerland). https://www.iso
               .org/standard/71952.html

[FIPS 199]   National Institute of Standards and Technology (2004) Standards for
               Security Categorization of Federal Information and Information Systems.
               (U.S. Department of Commerce, Washington, DC), Federal Information
               Processing Standards Publication (FIPS) 199. https://doi.org/10.6028/
               NIST.FIPS.199

[SP 800-30]   Joint Task Force Transformation Initiative (2012) Guide for Conducting
               Risk Assessments. (National Institute of Standards and Technology,
               Gaithersburg, MD), NIST Special Publication (SP) 800-30, Rev. 1.
               https://doi.org/10.6028/NIST.SP.800-30r1

[SP 800-34]   Swanson MA, Bowen P, Phillips AW, Gallup D, Lynes D (2010)
               Contingency Planning Guide for Federal Information Systems. (National
               Institute of Standards and Technology, Gaithersburg, MD), NIST Special
               Publication (SP) 800-34, Rev. 1, Includes updates as of November 11,
               2010. https://doi.org/10.6028/NIST.SP.800-34r1

[SP 800-37]   Joint Task Force (2018) Risk Management Framework for Information
               Systems and Organizations: A System Life Cycle Approach for
               Security and Privacy. (National Institute of Standards and Technology,
               Gaithersburg, MD), NIST Special Publication (SP) 800-37, Rev. 2.

               https://doi.org/10.6028/NIST.SP.800-37r2

[SP 800-39]   Joint Task Force Transformation Initiative (2011) Managing Information

               Security Risk: Organization, Mission, and Information System View.
               (National Institute of Standards and Technology, Gaithersburg, MD),
               NIST Special Publication (SP) 800-39.

               https://doi.org/10.6028/NIST.SP.800-39

[SP 800-53]   Joint Task Force Transformation Initiative (2020) Security and Privacy
               Controls for Information Systems and Organizations. (National Institute
               of Standards and Technology, Gaithersburg, MD), NIST Special
               Publication (SP) 800-53, Rev. 5, Includes updates as of December 10,
               2020. https://doi.org/10.6028/NIST.SP.800-53r5

[SP 800-53B]   Joint Task Force Transformation Initiative (2019) Control Baselines
               for Systems and Organizations. (National Institute of Standards and
               Technology, Gaithersburg, MD), NIST Special Publication (SP) 800-53B,
               Includes updates as of December 10, 2020. https://doi.org/10.6028/
               NIST.SP.800-53B

[SP 800-82] Stouffer KA, Lightman S, Pillitteri VY, Abrams M, Hahn A (2015) Guide to Industrial Control Systems (ICS) Security. (National Institute of Standards and Technology, Gaithersburg, MD), NIST Special Publication (SP) 800-82, Rev. 2.

https://doi.org/10.6028/NIST.SP.800-82r2

[SP 800-88] Kissel R, Regenscheid A, Scholl M, Stine K (2014) Guidelines for Media Sanitization. (National Institute of Standards and Technology, Gaithersburg, MD), NIST Special Publication (SP) 800-88, Rev. 1. https://doi.org/10.6028/NIST.SP.800-88r1

[SP 800-95] Singhal A, Winograd T, Scarfone KA (2007) Guide to Secure Web Services. (National Institute of Standards and Technology, Gaithersburg, MD), NIST Special Publication (SP) 800-95.

https://doi.org/10.6028/NIST.SP.800-95

[SP 800-125B] Chandramouli R (2016) Secure Virtual Network Configuration for Virtual Machine (VM) Protection. (National Institute of Standards and Technology, Gaithersburg, MD), NIST Special Publication (SP) 800-125B. https://doi.org/10.6028/NIST.SP.800-125B

[SP 800-160 v1] Ross RS, Oren JC, McEvilley M (2016) Systems Security Engineering: Considerations for a Multidisciplinary Approach in the Engineering of Trustworthy Secure Systems. (National Institute of Standards and Technology, Gaithersburg, MD), NIST Special Publication (SP) 800-160, Vol. 1, Includes updates as of March 21, 2018.

https://doi.org/10.6028/NIST.SP.800-160v1

[SP 800-161] Boyens JM, Paulsen C, Moorthy R, Bartol N (2015) Supply Chain Risk Management Practices for Federal Information Systems and Organizations. (National Institute of Standards and Technology, Gaithersburg, MD), NIST Special Publication (SP) 800-161.

https://doi.org/10.6028/NIST.SP.800-161

[SP 800-171] Ross RS, Dempsey KL, Viscuso P, Riddle M, Guissanie G (2016) Protecting

Controlled Unclassified Information in Nonfederal Systems and Organizations. (National Institute of Standards and Technology, Gaithersburg, MD), NIST Special Publication (SP) 800-171, Rev. 1, Includes updates as of June 7, 2018.

https://doi.org/10.6028/NIST.SP.800-171r1

[SP 800-183] Voas, J (2016) Networks of 'Things'. (National Institute of Standards and Technology, Gaithersburg, MD), NIST Special Publication (SP) 800-183. https://doi.org/10.6028/NIST.SP.800-183

[SP 800-207]   Rose S, Borchert O, Mitchell S, Connelly S (2020) Zero Trust
Architecture. (National Institute of Standards and Technology,
Gaithersburg, MD), NIST Special Publication (SP) 800-207.

https://doi.org/10.6028/NIST.SP.800-207

[SP 1500-201]   Burns MJ, Greer C, Griffor ER, Wollman DA (2017) Framework for
Cyber- Physical Systems: Volume 1, Overview, Version 1.0. (National
Institute of Standards and Technology, Gaithersburg, MD), NIST
Special Publication (SP) 1500-201.

https://doi.org/10.6028/NIST.SP.1500-201

[SP 1190]   Butry D, et al. (2016) Community Resilience Planning Guide for
Buildings and Infrastructure Systems, Volume I. (National Institute
of Standards and Technology, Gaithersburg, MD), NIST Special
Publication (SP) 1190, Vol. 1. https://doi.org/10.6028/NIST.SP.1190v1

[IR 8179]   Paulsen C, Boyens JM, Bartol N, Winkler K (2018) Criticality Analysis
Process Model: Prioritizing Systems and Components. (National
Institute of Standards and Technology, Gaithersburg, MD), NIST
Interagency or Internal Report (IR) 8179.

https://doi.org/10.6028/NIST.IR.8179

[IR 8202]   Yaga DJ, Mell PM, Roby N, Scarfone KA (2018) Blockchain Technology
Overview. (National Institute of Standards and Technology,
Gaithersburg, MD), NIST Interagency or Internal Report (IR) 8202.

https://doi.org/10.6028/NIST.IR.8202

[IR 8259]   Fagan M, Megas KN, Scarfone KA, Smith M (2019) Foundational
Cybersecurity Activities for IoT Device Manufacturers. (National Institute
of Standards and Technology, Gaithersburg, MD), NIST Interagency or
Internal Report (IR) 8259.

https://doi.org/10.6028/NIST.IR.8259

[IR 8286]   Stine K, Quinn S, Witte G, Gardner RK (2020) Integrating Cybersecurity
and Enterprise Risk Management (ERM). (National Institute of Standards
and Technology, Gaithersburg, MD), NIST Interagency or Internal
Report (IR) 8286.

https://doi.org/10.6028/NIST.IR.8286

[IR 8301]   Lesavre L, Varin P, Yaga D (2021) Blockchain Networks: Token Design
and Management Overview. National Institute of Standards and
Technology, Gaithersburg, MD), NIST Interagency or Internal Report
(IR) 8301.

https://doi.org/10.6028/NIST.IR.8301

[IR 8360]   Hu VC (2021) Machine Learning for Access Control Policy Verification.

(National Institute of Standards and Technology, Gaithersburg, MD),
NIST Interagency or Internal Report (IR) 8360. https://doi.org/10.6028/
NIST.IR.8360

[MIL-STD-882E] Department of Defense (2012) *MIL-STD-882E – Standard Practice: System Safety* (U.S. Department of Defense, Washington, DC). https:// www.dau.edu/cop/armyesoh/DAU%20Sponsored%20Documents/ MIL- STD-882E.pdf

Miscellaneous Publications and Websites

[Avizienis04] Avižienis A, Laprie JC, Randell B (2004) Dependability and Its Threats: A Taxonomy. *Building the Information Society, IFIP International Federation for Information Processing*, ed Jacquart R (Springer, Boston, MA), Vol. 156, pp 91–120.

https://doi.org/10.1007/978-1-4020-8157-6_13

[Bodeau11] Bodeau D, Graubart R (2011) Cyber Resiliency Engineering Framework, Version 1.0.

https://www.mitre.org/sites/default/files/pdf/11_4436.pdf

[Bodeau15] Bodeau D, Graubart R, Heinbockel W, Laderman E (2015) Cyber Resiliency Engineering Aid – The Updated Cyber Resiliency Engineering Framework and Guidance on Applying Cyber Resiliency Techniques. (The MITRE Corporation, Bedford, MA), MITRE Technical Report MTR-140499R1. http://www.mitre.org/sites/default/files/ publications/pr-15-1334-cyber- resiliency-engineering-aid-framework-update.pdf

[Bodeau16] Bodeau D, Graubart R (2016) Cyber Prep 2.0: Motivating Organizational Cyber Strategies in Terms of Threat Preparedness. (The MITRE Corporation, Bedford, MA), MITRE Technical Report MTR-150264. https://www.mitre.org/sites/default/files/publications/15-0797-cyber-prep-2- motivating-organizational-cyber-strategies.pdf

[Bodeau17] Bodeau D, Graubart R (2017) Cyber Resiliency Design Principles: Selective Use Throughout the Life Cycle and in Conjunction with Related Disciplines. (The MITRE Corporation, Bedford, MA), MITRE Technical Report MTR- 170001.

https://www.mitre.org/sites/default/files/publications/PR%20 17- 0103%20Cyber%20Resiliency%20Design%20Principles%20 MTR17001.pdf

[Bodeau18a] Bodeau DJ, McCollum CD, Fox DB (2018) Cyber Threat Modeling: Survey, Assessment, and Representative Framework. (The MITRE Corporation, McLean, VA), PR 18-1174.

https://www.mitre.org/sites/default/files/publications/pr_18-1174-ngci-cyber-threat-modeling.pdf

[Bodeau18b]   Bodeau D, Graubart R, McQuaid R, Woodill J (2018) Cyber Resiliency Metrics, Measures of Effectiveness, and Scoring: Enabling Systems Engineers and Program Managers to Select the Most Useful Assessment Methods. (The MITRE Corporation, Bedford, MA), MITRE Technical Report MTR-180314.

https://www.mitre.org/sites/default/files/publications/pr-18-2579-cyber- resiliency-metrics-measures-of-effectiveness-and-scoring.pdf

[Bodeau21]   Bodeau D, Graubart R, Jones LK, Laderman E (2021). Cyber Resiliency Approaches and Controls to Mitigate Adversary Tactics, Techniques, and Procedures (TTPs): Mapping Cyber Resiliency to the ATT&CK® Framework

– Revision 2. (The MITRE Corporation, Bedford, MA), MITRE Technical Report MTR-200286R2.

[Brtis16]   Brtis J (2016) How to Think about Resilience in a DoD Context. (The MITRE Corporation, Colorado Springs, CO), MITRE Technical Report MTR-160138.

[CISA HVA]   Cybersecurity and Infrastructure Security Agency, *Secure High Value Assets.*

https://www.cisa.gov/publication/secure-high-value-assets

[Clemen13]   Clemen RT, Reilly T (2013) *Making Hard Decisions with the Decision Tools Suite* (South-Western Cengage Learning, Mason, OH), 3rd Ed., pp 848.

[DHS10]   Department of Homeland Security Risk Steering Committee (2010) DHS Risk Lexicon. (U.S. Department of Homeland Security, Washington, DC), 2010 Edition.

https://www.dhs.gov/xlibrary/assets/dhs-risk-lexicon-2010.pdf

[DHSCDM]   Department of Homeland Security, "CDM Program What is .govCAR?"

https://www.cisa.gov/sites/default/files/publications/2020%2009%20 03_%20CDM%20Program%20govCAR_Fact%20Sheet_2.pdf

[DOD20]   Department of Defense, "Department of Defense Cybersecurity Test and Evaluation Guidebook," Version 2.0, Change 1, February 2020.

https://www.dau.edu/cop/test/DAU%20Sponsored%20Documents/ Cybersecurity-Test-and-Evaluation-Guidebook-Version2-change-1.pdf

[DOD16]   Department of Defense (2016) Mission Assurance (U.S. Department of Defense, Washington, DC), DoD Directive (DODD) 3020.40. https:// www.esd.whs.mil/Portals/54/Documents/DD/issuances/dodd/302040p. pdf?ver=2018-09-11-131221-983

[DSB13]   Defense Science Board (2013) Resilient Military Systems and the Advanced Cyber Threat. (U.S. Department of Defense, Washington, DC). https://dsb.cto.mil/reports/2010s/ ResilientMilitarySystemsCyberThreat.pdf

[Folk15]   Folk C, Hurley DC, Kaplow WK, Payne JF (2015) The Security
               Implications of the Internet of Things. (AFCEA International Cyber
               Committee). https://www.afcea.org/site/sites/default/files/files/AFC_
               WhitePaper_Revised_Out.pdf

[GAO18]   Government Accountability Office (2018) Weapon Systems
               Cybersecurity.

               (Government Accountability Office, Washington, DC), GAO-19-128,
               October 2018.

               https://www.gao.gov/assets/700/694913.pdf

[Heckman15]   Heckman KE, Stech FJ, Thomas RK, Schmoder B, Tsow AW (2015)
               Cyber Denial, Deception and Counter Deception: A Framework for
               Supporting Active Cyber Defense, *Advances in Information Security*
               (Springer, Cham, Switzerland), Vol. 63.

[Höller15]   Höller A, Rauter T, Iber J, Kreiner C (2015) Towards Dynamic Software
               Diversity for Resilient Redundant Embedded Systems. *Proceedings of
               Software Engineering for Resilient Systems: 7th International Workshop,
               SERENE 2015* (Springer, Paris, France), pp 16–30.

               https://doi.org/10.1007/978-3-319-23129-7_2

[Hutchins11]   Hutchins EM, Cloppert MJ, Amin RM (2011) Intelligence-driven
               computer network defense informed by analysis of adversary
               campaigns and intrusion kill chains. *Leading Issues in Information
               Warfare & Security Research*, ed Ryan J (Academic Publishing
               International, Reading, UK), Vol. 1, pp 78–104.

[IEEE90]   Institute of Electrical and Electronics Engineers (1990) *IEEE Standard
               Computer Dictionary: A Compilation of IEEE Standard Computer
               Glossaries*, (IEEE, New York, NY).

[IEEE17]   Institute of Electrical and Electronics Engineers, Association for
               Computing Machinery (2017) *Enterprise IT Body of Knowledge –
               Glossary. Enterprise IT Body of Knowledge.*

               http://eitbokwiki.org/Glossary#eit

[INCOSE11]   International Council for Systems Engineering (2011) *Resilient Systems
               Working Group Charter.* (INCOSE, San Diego, CA).

[INCOSE14]   International Council on Systems Engineering (2015) *System
               Engineering Handbook—A Guide for System Engineering Life Cycle
               Processes and Activities.* (John Wiley & Sons, Hoboken, NJ), 4th Ed.

[ISACA]   ISACA (2019) *ISACA Glossary of Terms.*

               https://www.isaca.org/pages/glossary.aspx

[Jackson07]   Jackson S (2007) A Multidisciplinary Framework for Resilience to
               Disasters and Disruptions. *Transactions of the Society for Design and
               Process Science* 11(2):91-108.

[Jackson13]   Jackson S, Ferris T (2013) Resilience Principles for Engineered Systems. *Systems Engineering* 16(2): 152-164.

[Jajodia11]   Jajodia S, Ghosh AK, Swarup V, Wang C, Wang XS (eds.) (2011) *Moving Target Defense: Creating Asymmetric Uncertainty for Cyber Threats* (Springer-Verlag, New York, NY), Advances in Information Security, Vol. 54, pp 184.

               https://doi.org/10.1007/978-1-4614-0977-9

[Jajodia12]   Jajodia S, Ghosh AK, Subrahmanian VS, Swarup V, Wang C, Wang XS (eds.) (2013) *Moving Target Defense II: Application of Game Theory and Adversarial Modeling* (Springer-Verlag, New York, NY), Advances in Information Security, Vol. 100, pp 204.

[JCS17]   Joint Chiefs of Staff (2017) Cyber Survivability Endorsement Implementation Guide (CSEIG). (U.S. Department of Defense, Washington, DC), v1.01.

[King12]   King S (2012) *National and Defense S&T Strategies & Initiatives.*

[Leveson12]   Leveson NG (2012) *Engineering a Safer World: Systems Thinking Applied to Safety* (MIT Press, Cambridge, MA), pp 560.

[Madni07]   Madni AM (2007) Designing for Resilience. *ISTI Lecture Notes on Advanced Topics in Systems Engineering* (University of California at Los Angeles (UCLA), Los Angeles, CA).

[Madni09]   Madni AM, Jackson S (2009) Towards a Conceptual Framework for Resilience Engineering, *IEEE Systems Journal* 3(2):181-191.

[MITRE07]   The MITRE Corporation (2019) *Common Attack Pattern Enumeration and Classification (CAPEC).*

               https://capec.mitre.org/index.html

[MITRE18]   The MITRE Corporation (2018) *Adversarial Tactics, Techniques & Common Knowledge (ATT&CK™).*

               https://attack.mitre.org

[MITRE21]   The MITRE Corporation (2021) CALDERA™: A Scalable, Automated Adversary Emulation Platform.

               https://caldera.mitre.org

[Musman18]   Musman S, Agbolosu-Amison S, Crowther K (2019) Metrics Based on the Mission Risk Perspective. *Cyber Resilience of Systems and Networks*, eds Kott A, Linkov I (Springer International Publishing, Cham, Switzerland) Chapter 3, pp 41–65.

               https://doi.org/10.1007/978-3-319-77492-3

[NASA19]   National Aeronautics and Space Administration (2019) Systems Engineering Handbook, Section 6.4: Technical Risk Management. https://www.nasa.gov/seh/6-4-technical-risk-management

[Neumann04]   Neumann P (2004) Principled Assuredly Trustworthy Composable
               Architectures. (SRI International, Menlo Park, CA), CDRL A001 Final
               Report. http://www.csl.sri.com/users/neumann/chats4.pdf

[NIAC10]   National Infrastructure Advisory Council (NIAC) (2010) A Framework
               for Establishing Critical Infrastructure Resilience Goals: Final Report
               and Recommendations by the Council. (U.S. Department of Homeland
               Security, Washington, DC).

               https://www.dhs.gov/xlibrary/assets/niac/niac-a-framework-for-
               establishing-critical-infrastructure-resilience-goals-2010-10-19.pdf

[NIST16]   National Institute of Standards and Technology Workshop (2016)
               *Exploring the Dimensions of Trustworthiness: Challenges and
               Opportunities.*

               https://www.nist.gov/news-events/events/2016/08/exploring-
               dimensions- trustworthiness-challenges-and-opportunities

[NIST CSF]   National Institute of Standards and Technology (2018) Framework for
               Improving Critical Infrastructure Cybersecurity, Version 1.1. (National
               Institute of Standard, Gaithersburg, MD). https://doi.org/10.6028/NIST.
               CSWP.04162018

[ODNI17]   Office of the Director of National Intelligence (2017) *Cyber Threat
               Framework.*

               https://www.dni.gov/index.php/cyber-threat-framework

[Okhravi13]   Okhravi H, Rabe MA, Mayberry TJ, Leonard WG, Hobson TR, Bigelow
               D, Streilein WW (2013) Survey of Cyber Moving Targets. (Lincoln
               Laboratory, Lexington, MA), Technical Report 1166. http://web.mit
               .edu/ha22286/www/papers/LLTechRep.pdf

[Pitcher19]   Pitcher S (2019) New DoD Approaches on the Cyber Survivability of
               Weapon Systems [presentation].

               https://www.itea.org/wp-content/uploads/2019/03/Pitcher-Steve.pdf

[Pitcher21]   Pitcher S, Andress T (2021) Cyber Survivability for Future and Legacy
               DoD Weapon Systems [presentation].

               https://www.ndia.org/-/media/sites/ndia/divisions/systems-
               engineering/se--- june-2021-meeting/cse-support-to-future-and-legacy-
               dod-systems-10-jun-2021- for-ndia.ashx

[Reilly19]   Reilly J (2019) *Cyber Survivability Attributes: CSA Tool (8ABW-
               2019-2267)* (Air Force Research Laboratory, Rome, NY).

[Ricci14]   Ricci N, Rhodes DH, Ross AM (2014) Evolvability-Related Options in
               Military Systems of Systems. *Procedia Computer Science* 28:314-321.

               https://doi.org/10.1016/j.procs.2014.03.039

[Richards08]   Richards MG, Ross AM, Hastings DE, Rhodes DH (2008) Empirical
                Validation of Design Principles for Survivable System Architecture.
                Proceedings of the 2nd Annual IEEE Systems Conference, (IEEE,
                Montreal, Quebec, Canada), pp 1–8.

                https://doi.org/10.1109/SYSTEMS.2008.4518999

[Richards09]   Richards MG, Hastings DE, Rhodes DH, Ross AM, Weigel AL (2009)
                Design for Survivability: Concept Generation and Evaluation in
                Dynamic Tradespace Exploration. *Second International Symposium
                on Engineering Systems* (Massachusetts Institute of Technology,
                Cambridge, MA). https://pdfs.semanticscholar.org/3734/7b58123c16e
                84e2f51a4e172ddee0a8755c0.pdf

[SEBoK]   BKCASE Editorial Board (2019) The Guide to the Systems Engineering
                Body of Knowledge (SEBoK), v. 2.0, ed Cloutier RJ (The Trustees of the
                Stevens Institute of Technology, Hoboken, NJ). BKCASE is managed
                and maintained by the Stevens Institute of Technology Systems
                Engineering Research Center, the International Council on Systems
                Engineering, and the Institute of Electrical and Electronics Engineers
                Computer Society. https://www.sebokwiki.org/wiki/Guide_to_the_
                Systems_Engineering_Body_of_Knowledge_(SEBoK)

[Sheard08]   Sheard S (2008) A Framework for System Resilience Discussions.
                INCOSE International Symposium 18 (Wiley, Utrecht, The Netherlands),
                pp 1243–1257.

                https://doi.org/10.1002/j.2334-5837.2008.tb00875.x

[Shetty16]   Shetty S, Yuchi X, Song M (2016) *Moving Target Defense for
                Distributed Systems* (Springer International, Switzerland), pp 76.

                https://doi.org/10.1007/978-3-319-31032-9

[Sterbenz06]   Sterbenz J, Hutchinson D (2006) ResiliNets: Multilevel Resilient and
                Survivable Networking Initiative.

[Sterbenz10]   Sterbenz JPG, Hutchison D, Çetinkaya EK, Jabbar A, Rohrer JP,
                Schöller M, Smith P (2010) Resilience and survivability in communication
                networks: Strategies, principles, and survey of disciplines. *Computer
                Networks* 54:1245–1265.

                http://www.ittc.ku.edu/resilinets/papers/Sterbenz-Hutchison-Cetinkaya-
                Jabbar- Rohrer-Scholler-Smith-2010.pdf

[Sterbenz14]   Sterbenz JP, Hutchison D, Çetinkaya EK, Jabbar A, Rohrer JP, Schöller
                M, Smith P (2014) Redundancy, diversity, and connectivity to achieve
                multilevel network resilience, survivability, and disruption tolerance.
                Journal of Telecommunications Systems 56(1):17–31.

                https://doi.org/10.1007/s11235-013-9816-9

[Strom17]   Strom BE, Battaglia JA, Kemmerer MS, Kupersanin W, Miller DP,
              Wampler C, Whitley SM, Wolf RD (2017) Finding Cyber Threats with
              ATT&CK-Based Analytics. (The MITRE Corporation, Annapolis Junction,
              MD), MITRE Technical Report MTR-170202. https://www.mitre.org/
              sites/default/files/publications/16-3713-finding-cyber- threats%20
              with%20att%26ck-based-analytics.pdf

[Temin10]   Temin A, Musman S (2010) A Language for Capturing Cyber Impact
              Effects. (The MITRE Corporation, Bedford, MA), MITRE Technical
              Report MTR- 100344.

[Zimmerman14] Zimmerman C (2014) Ten Strategies of a World-Class Cybersecurity
              Operations Center. (The MITRE Corporation, Bedford, MA). http://
              www.mitre.org/sites/default/files/publications/pr-13-1028-mitre-10-
              strategies-cyber-ops-center.pdf

Index

Page numbers followed by *f* and *t* refer to figures and tables, respectively.